Pilgrim in the Holy Land

Pilgrim
in the Holy Land

A JOURNEY WITH
DAME THORA HIRD

Rob Marshall

Illustrations and maps by
Taffy Davies

DARTON · LONGMAN + TODD

First published in 1995 by
Darton, Longman and Todd Ltd
1 Spencer Court
140–142 Wandsworth High Street
London SW18 4JJ

ISBN 0–232–52112–3

A catalogue record for this book is available
from the British Library.

Text design by Sandie Boccacci
Cover design by Judy Linard

Phototypeset in 12/13½pt Garamond by Intype, London
Printed and bound in Great Britain by
BPC Wheatons Ltd, Exeter

Acknowledgements

I have visited the Holy Land many times in the past but my pilgrimage with Dame Thora Hird and her family was memorable for so many reasons. The idea for this book came about over dinner on our second night in Jerusalem. 'If ever you write a book about how this land can help us in our daily lives back home, I'll help you,' said Thora. Dame Thora has spent many hours reflecting on her holiday. I am grateful to her, to her late husband, Jimmy, and to her daughter, Jan, for their loving help and support.

Thanks must also go to Mr René Siva and all at Fairlink Christian Travel for their excellent organisation of the tour itself, to El Al (Israel) Airlines for looking after Thora's family so well, and to Leon our guide and all the team in the Holy Land who made it such a wonderful pilgrimage.

Finally, thanks are due to my editor, Morag Reeve, to Taffy Davies for the wonderful cartoons and to all who have made the book so attractive in its design and layout.

Contents

Contents

Contents

List of Illustrations

Introduction

After almost two decades in religious broadcasting, Dame Thora Hird is used to being asked questions about her faith. Why do you believe in God? What way do you find easiest to pray? What about all the suffering in the world? During two eventful weeks in the Holy Land Thora was able to pull together many of the strands in her own mind and heart concerning faith and belief today.

This is not a guide book (though it will be of value to anyone visiting the Holy Land) but it is one which I believe many people, including pilgrims to the Holy Land, will find useful because of Thora's wonderful insights and wisdom. She brings the great events of faith and love into sharp focus for today. Certainly, if you are planning to visit Israel, I am sure that you will enjoy taking Thora with you in the form of this book.

For each major site or place which we visited there is a record of the reading we heard, the hymn we sang and the prayer we prayed. We have dealt only with the main sites; lesser venues have had to be omitted through shortage of space.

This book gives you the chance to travel in the footsteps of Jesus with one of Britain's best-loved actresses and religious broadcasters. It is full of Thora's wisdom and wit, which I know you will enjoy.

ROB MARSHALL *London, 1995*

Part One

On the Way

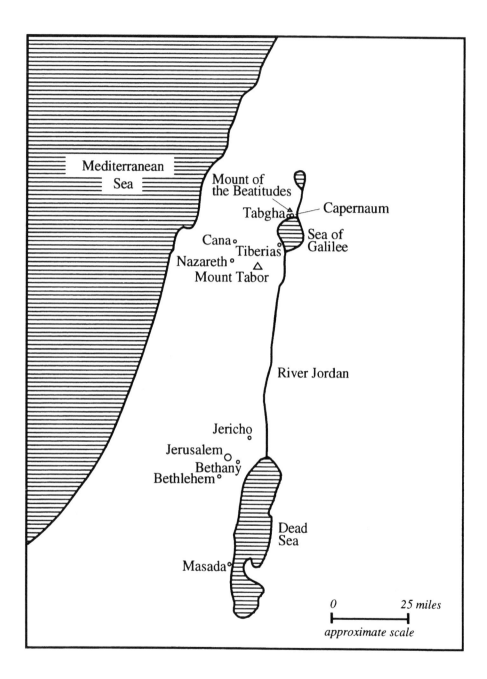

Mediterranean
Sea

Mount of
the Beatitudes

Tabgha

Capernaum

Cana

Tiberias

Sea of
Galilee

Nazareth

Mount Tabor

River Jordan

Jericho

Jerusalem

Bethany

Bethlehem

Dead
Sea

Masada

0   25 miles

approximate scale

1

Just One of the Group

A UNIQUE JOURNEY

I first met Thora Hird when she was filming a sequence
with the Bishop of London in his Westminster home. He
was to be a guest on her 'Praise Be!' programme. The after-
noon went very well and we had a lot of time to chat and

get to know one another. Just before she was due to leave I remember asking her, 'Thora, would you like to use the bathroom before you go?' She smiled, laughed out loud and said, 'I can tell you're a northern lad. Only a northerner would ask that ... but, yes, I'd love to.'

We then met socially a few times and I was pleased to be introduced to her husband, James Scott (Scottie), in their lovely mews home in central London. Scottie was a gracious and thoroughly reliable gentleman who had been a constant support to Thora over the years. He was always there but not always obvious. They were a remarkable couple. Scottie died five months after our pilgrimage. This was one of Thora and Scottie's last overseas trips together and, in Thora's words, 'there could have been none better'.

In a chance conversation just two months before it was announced by Buckingham Palace in 1994 that Thora was to become a Dame, I was telling her about my annual pilgrimage to the Holy Land. 'Do you know,' she replied, 'that's something I've always wanted to do. A proper pilgrimage – without a film crew and all that, but a chance to go in the footsteps of Jesus and visit the lovely places that I have read about from Sunday School days.'

Dame Thora had laid down a challenge. A special itinerary was put together by Fairlink Christian Travel in South Kensington. A double-decker bus would be hired and we would aim at taking seventy pilgrims with us. Thora and Scottie would be joined by their daughter, Janette Scott, a retired Hollywood actress who was known by everyone in the group. It was quite an undertaking.

The 'Hird party' were to fly out two days before the group. Thora's pilgrims would meet them for the first time on the shores of the Sea of Galilee. Thora and Scottie were delighted with the plans. 'Just treat us like one of the group,' they kept on saying. But I knew just how much the pilgrims were looking forward to sharing their faith and experiences with one of the best-loved and most respected actresses in Britain today. It would be a journey to remember!

Thora kept notes of her feelings and responses to the many places of pilgrimage. I interviewed her immediately after we returned and the reflections recorded in this book are taken from those interviews. She links up her profound faith in a God of love with her experience of life; she connects biblical events and happenings with the great Christian seasons; she also laughs about life and living. At the same time, she was often overcome by the sheer emotion of all that she saw and heard. All this comes out in her thoughts throughout the book. Each chapter has a brief description of the site we visited, a reading, a reflection by Thora on what she saw and experienced, together with the prayer we used and the hymn we sang, both introduced by Thora. The emphasis is indeed on Thora and on her own faith, wisdom and wit.

Dame Thora reflects

"Looking back now, I thought the pilgrimage was marvellous. I am still taking it all in. It was only afterwards when I was sitting at home with Jimmy (God bless him) that I began to ask myself – was I good enough for this? It isn't an acting job, so it was a wonderful opportunity and I would say to everyone that a pilgrimage to the Holy Land is the gilt edge around your faith. As far as I can see, once you have been on a pilgrimage, you don't doubt any of the basics any more. It was joyous for me.

I had been once before to the Holy Land and the background to Jesus from Sunday School was always there then. But this time, because of the readings and hymns and the lovely people who joined us, I felt that we were in the right place. There was nothing on the

pilgrimage that did not impress me. Not one detail. And
I learnt so much.   **"**

Our prayer as we set off
May the Lord bless you and watch over you;
May the Lord make his face shine upon you and be gracious
   to you;
May the Lord look kindly on you and give you peace.

A pilgrim's prayer
Lord Jesus,
on this pilgrimage,
help us to discover more about you.
Enable us to understand your word,
reveal your love and purpose to us in the sacraments,
and keep us from falling into sin.
Guide and protect us in all that we discover
and challenge us to be more effective disciples when we
   return home.
For your name's sake.
Amen.

2

One Sip Is Enough!

THE BIRTHDAY FLIGHT

There was genuine excitement when we left Thora's London home. Scottie was keen to make sure that everything was packed into the car, whilst Jan double checked that the house was securely locked. Thora was looking forward to the flight and to meeting the group once we had settled down. After a ride from Marble Arch to London's Heathrow Airport there would be the traditional security and baggage checks before boarding the plane. Then, after a flight lasting about five hours, we were to be met in Tel Aviv by Leon Segal, our guide for the ten-day tour. He would drive the Hird party to the lakeside town of Tiberias. I would wait for Thora's pilgrims at Ben Gurion Airport, where they would arrive thirty-six hours later.

At Heathrow we proceeded through the usual series of checks and counter-checks. It was an amusing moment to see Thora being interviewed by the security officers at the airport.

Q: Who packed your suitcase?
A: Well, we did, together, because I can't trust Jimmy to put everything in properly . . .
Q: Do you know anyone in Israel?
A: No, darling, no one I could mention.
Q: Do you carry any weapon with you?
A: Oh nooo! Me? No, darling!
Q: Has your suitcase been with you all the time?
A: Yes it has, well, it's been with the dog collar. I mean he has been with us all the time! (Big smile)
Q: OK, Dame Thora. Please don't accept anything from anyone before boarding the flight and have a nice flight.

We went into the King David Lounge in the El Al hospitality area and enjoyed coffee and biscuits before the flight was eventually called. And it turned out to be quite a flight. A few of our fellow travellers came over to congratulate Thora on becoming a Dame, and the lady on duty in the lounge even asked if she could have a picture taken with Dame Thora. The excitement was mounting.

Dame Thora reflects
"We travelled out to the Holy Land, two days before my

22

eighty-third birthday, on board an El Al 'Jumbo'. I suppose we had been in the air for about forty-five minutes when this stewardess came along with a tray containing a large bottle of champagne and two glasses. It was for my birthday. 'Happy birthday, Dame Thora,' she said. What I should have said was that it wasn't my birthday on that day, but all I thought was, 'Oh, they have gone to all this trouble'.

Now then, neither my husband nor I could drink a whole bottle of champagne. In fact, one sip is enough! So the people in front were prodded, along with the people in the aisles: 'Do you fancy a sip of champers?' They looked a bit surprised. But they enjoyed a celebration with us.

A few minutes later a stewardess turned up again, this time with a basket of fruit. All different fruits from the Holy Land, of course! Oranges, bananas, the most lovely grapes, dates and nuts. Ten minutes later a birthday cake came, made entirely of chocolate. It was lovely of them.

Now, there's not much room in an aircraft seat to drink champagne and eat fruit and a delicious cake. But I was celebrating and it was lovely. Of course, at the end of it, I had chocolate all over my jumper and trousers – there was hardly any room to move, holding it all like that – and Jimmy got it on his suit. But who cares? Everyone was happy as we went towards the Holy Land. We were already celebrating. It was so nice and loving. It helped us get to know strangers. The landing was excellent and when the plane door opened you could feel the balmy air and smell the palm trees of Tel Aviv.

We went through customs and met Leon our guide. It was *love* from arriving there. That is what we met –

pure love. Our guide had been in the army for a long time and his knowledge of the land was incredible. Leon was humorous and brilliant as a guide. Everything was 'no problem' and he really meant that it was no problem. We were in a lovely double-decker bus with a television screen so that the guide and the driver – whom I called Spartacus because he had such a handsome profile – could keep an eye on what was going on upstairs!

The guide would explain something and then shout, 'Are you all awake up there?' And that would shock them. We travelled everywhere on our double-decker bus. It became known as Dame Thora's Bus. We must have got on and off it more than a hundred times, sometimes for quite a while and other times just to admire the view or take a picture. We went north and south, east and west. It became our home for ten days. **"**

3

Where God Has Called His People

UNDERSTANDING THE LAND
OF JESUS

The Holy Land is an exciting place to visit. Of all the countries in the world, there is something special about the people and places of the Middle East which gives them a charm of their very own. It is a land of beauty and desert.

The stark saltiness of the Dead Sea contrasts vividly with the fresh Sea of Galilee and the running water of the River Jordan. There are mountains and hills as well as stunning valleys of freshly planted forests. Flowers blossom throughout the year and plants yielding aromatic herbs and spices grow in abundance. Birds from Europe and Africa meet at the Syrian–African rift. It is a land of great contrasts.

Once you have left Ben Gurion Airport on your way either to Tiberias or to Jerusalem, you cannot fail to be aware that this is a special land. Road signs are written in Hebrew, English and Arabic. I remember, on my first visit, experiencing real exhilaration when I saw a sign to Jerusalem for the first time. Was I really so close to the Holy City? The road climbs steadily from Tel Aviv to Jerusalem: it is a dramatic approach.

Place names like Nazareth, Jericho and Bethlehem are around every corner. The Bible names come to life. You really are here – in the land of the pilgrims. What will immediately strike the visitor is the way in which the countryside is so rich in green, fertile areas. Israel now has a National Parks Authority which looks after more than forty sites.

Since the foundation of Israel in 1948 the Jewish community has attempted to build a modern, thriving state amongst the historical sites of their ancient land. They have developed an intricate water-supply system with excellent irrigation. Gas and electricity supplies have been brought to the villages and solar power is becoming widely available. The road network has been radically improved, reducing journey times from north to south, and from east to west. There is now a railway line between Tel Aviv and Jerusalem which is becoming increasingly popular. The national bus company (Egged) runs a comprehensive service to all of the major destinations. The taxi network is also impressive, with

26

The beautifully green countryside of Galilee

sheroot taxis (each taking up to twelve passengers) allowing people to share the ride from, say, Tel Aviv to Haifa or Jerusalem to Netanya for a cost that is less than the bus fare.

Relationships between Jew and Arab have been the subject of so many books and articles that it is difficult to sum it up for the pilgrim in any easy way. But it is important that anyone visiting the Holy Land understands that land has regularly changed hands between the two communities over the centuries and enmity and misunderstanding are always rife. As Dame Thora's party arrived there had been historic scenes in Jericho as Yasser Arafat, Chairman of the Palestine Liberation Organisation, had been welcomed back to the West Bank after more than two decades of campaigning for the Gaza Strip and the West Bank to be given back to the Palestinian community from the Israelis. Jericho was now being policed by the Palestinian police force, but a long-term solution to the geographical problems is still being sought. The West Bank and Gaza are inhabited by people who interpret the Arab cause in different ways, just as there is little consensus in Israel as to how far the Government should go in giving back previously won land. This tension is always around you but somehow you are never totally aware of the extent of it.

The growing range and quality of mass media (spoken, written and visual) has transformed life in Israel. Mobile phones, fax machines and video recorders are everywhere. There is a staple diet of news and information as politics and international relations continually dominate the headlines across the world.

Religion and culture are intertwined but not inseparable. The three main religions practised in the region – Judaism, Christianity and Islam – all have their place within the confines of the modern Israeli state. But the different expressions of all three religions within each of the communities make it a fascinating place to live or to visit. For example, Jews approach shabbat (the sabbath) in different ways; there are arguments between Christian denominations as to the true sites of Christian pilgrimage; within Islam there are different practices amongst various groupings. Consensus in religion is not always obvious! In his book *Behind the Star*, Gerald Butt, a BBC correspondent in Jerusalem, writes: 'Religion in the Middle East is inescapable; it is woven into the fabric of every hour that passes and of every action that is taken. Individuals, families, and whole sections in Middle Eastern societies will vary considerably in the degree to which they perform religious rituals to obey religious orders, but religion is a guiding hand for the majority. At times it is visible, at times it is not. And though religion can be a comforter, it can also excite dangerous passions.'

The villages and towns are diverse. You can tell a Muslim town by the tower (minaret) and dome of the mosque. Those towns without a mosque are usually Jewish or, very rarely, Christian. Types of housing range from apartment blocks and maisonettes in the major cities to the traditional-style individual dwellings that still dominate the landscape of the small villages. It is a land with a rich diversity of people, with varied cultures and languages.

Shops in the Holy Land often appear unattractive. Window dressing has not yet been invented there and it is the goods rather than the way in which they are presented which appeals most! Food shops vary according to local religious practices but there are some good supermarkets in the major towns. As pilgrims, we come across souvenir shops more than any other type and these vary in price rather than in the kind or quality of goods which they stock.

The threat of trouble or terrorist attacks is limited to certain geographical areas. Sadly, the local people have grown accustomed to hearing of injury, death and destruction. When you travel in a taxi or even on a bus you find that everyone goes quiet on the hour when the latest news bulletin is transmitted. The news has a function: it is about life and living.

A remarkable feature of the Holy Land is its topography. Israel has everything – fresh water, desert, mountains, valleys, forests and good agricultural land. The water of the Holy Land forms the focus in any map of the region: in the north is the Sea of Galilee from which the River Jordan flows south to the Dead Sea. Syria is to be found to the north, over the Golan Heights. Jordan, with whom a Peace Treaty was signed in 1994, is along the east side. Lebanon borders to the north-west and to the south of that is the Mediterranean coastline. Down near Elat at the southern tip of Israel is the meeting place of Egypt, Jordan, Saudi Arabia and Israel. Distances between the various sites and places are relatively small but the variety of landscape is impressive. Temperatures are obviously on the warm side, although from December to February in the Jerusalem area it can be very cold and often wet. The rest of the year sees a fairly hot and agreeable climate in Tel Aviv, even hotter weather in Jericho and along the Dead Sea, with Galilee and Jerusalem enjoying slightly cooler and often more comfortable climates.

The people of the Holy Land are also unique. There is a kind of mentality which it is difficult to convey to anyone who has not been there. The approach to life, work, the family and the future is a fascinating one. Everyone must work; nothing can be taken for granted; life must be lived to the full. Jewish men tend to be hard and enduring in their manner; they can often appear arrogant to a European mind. Arab men are much quieter on the whole but their sense of 'togetherness' within the family means that you are usually dealing with several people when you think you are dealing

A close-up view of the salt deposits of the Dead Sea
(see Postscript)

with one! Both Arab and Jewish women have traditional family roles which other western societies have been challenging over recent years. Feminism is not widespread but it does exist. Children look to the family for their future.

Dame Thora reflects

❝I have been very lucky in my life to travel to many different countries and I have always enjoyed seeing new places and new things. But to be in the Holy Land is a great experience. To actually think, 'I am here where God has called his people for centuries and centuries' is a wonderful thing.

I was impressed with the people we met – so full of life and purpose despite problems at times. I enjoyed the variety of the countryside, from the Dead Sea region and Masada to the beautifully green Galilee. I enjoyed it all, as you will see. **❞**

Our Hymn

❝Whenever we were in our double-decker looking out over the hills and mountains and the waters of the Holy Land I often thought of this hymn that many of us must have sung at Sunday School. It is a hymn which thanks God for his creation, for all the beauty that we see around us. It was written at the beginning of the last century by the wife of the Archbishop of Ireland because she wanted to help children to understand the Christian faith. But her lovely hymn – which I used to have sung regularly on the television – is very much for adults as well. **❞**

All things bright and beautiful,
All creatures great and small,
All things wise and wonderful,
The Lord God made them all.

Each little flower that opens,
Each little bird that sings,
He made their glowing colours,
He made their tiny wings.

The purple-headed mountain,
The river running by,
The sunset, and the morning,
That brightens up the sky.

The cold wind in the winter,
The pleasant summer sun,
The ripe fruits in the garden,
He made them every one.

The tall trees in the greenwood,
The meadows where we play,
The rushes by the water
We gather every day.

He gave us eyes to see them,
And lips that we might tell
How great is God Almighty
Who has made all things well.

(Mrs C. F. Alexander, 1823–95)

4

A Tiny Speck

MEETING THE PILGRIMS
IN GALILEE

Thora, Scottie and Jan were waiting in Tiberias. When I arrived at the airport to collect the pilgrims, I met our driver and saw the double-decker bus. It was the first time that Egged, the national coach company in Israel, had used a double-decker bus for a pilgrim party and there was a good deal of interest from other drivers and guides who wanted to have a look around. In fact, as the smart bus trundled around the little villages of the Holy Land many people would stop and stare and point at Dame Thora's bus as it arrived in their village square. It was amazing – a bus with two floors!

At exactly 6.30 am the first pilgrims arrived. They looked tired but happy. For many it was their first visit to the Holy Land. For several it had been their first flight. It really was wonderful to meet such a diverse group of people. 'How's Thora?' one shouted. 'Is Thora OK?' said another. I already knew that they would be very excited when they met her later that day. But first we had a two-and-a-half-hour journey to Tiberias where we had to settle in our hotel and have a sleep before boarding our boat to cross the Sea of Galilee. Thora, Scottie and Jan would be waiting for us. We all had to acclimatise to temperatures of 92°F. Most of the group dozed off on the coach. I pointed out some famous landmarks along the way. The pilgrimage had begun: together, we were to follow the life of Jesus and meet people of many faiths.

Dame Thora reflects

"We travelled around the Sea of Galilee before the group had actually met us. There was Scottie, Jan and myself, along with Domenico who helped me along if the going got tough. The group came to meet us at En Gev, a small kibbutz on the other side of the sea. And we waited for them there. It was very warm. Most of the time in May the temperature was around 30°C. But it wasn't a tiring kind of heat. There always seemed to be a gentle breeze – a nice, refreshing bit of fresh air.

The scenery around the Sea of Galilee is breathtaking. The mountains, the hills, the towns and the villages.

And none of the distances seemed very far, though the places looked a long way off much of the time. It was around these shores that Jesus walked. There we were on the side of the Sea and Jan said, 'Look, Mum, there's the boat.' Well, it was a tiny speck – a little boat in the middle of all that water. So we started waving at them just in case. And it seemed to get nearer so quickly. It was just like welcoming relatives. The kissing and cuddling and the lovely things people said. It was also nice because there was no embarrassment. They were people whom I had never met before and there we were greeting each other like cousins. It was something I will always be thankful for. The friendship was real and we were to share our time together. I felt as if I had already met them all.

I can see some of the faces even now. Millie sat behind us. She was mature in years, like me, but she was also amazing. With her lovely daughter, I don't think she missed out on anything. There were young children with their parents, a lady from Nigeria who had settled in London, someone who had nursed me quite a few years ago, and an Anglican vicar called John. All sorts of people, young and old, black and white, Catholic and Protestant, but we all got on so well: there wasn't one bit of division or trouble. We were led by Leon and Rob (the dog collar and author of this book) – quite a double act, those two.

We were off in the footsteps of Jesus! **"**

PART TWO

The Galilee Region

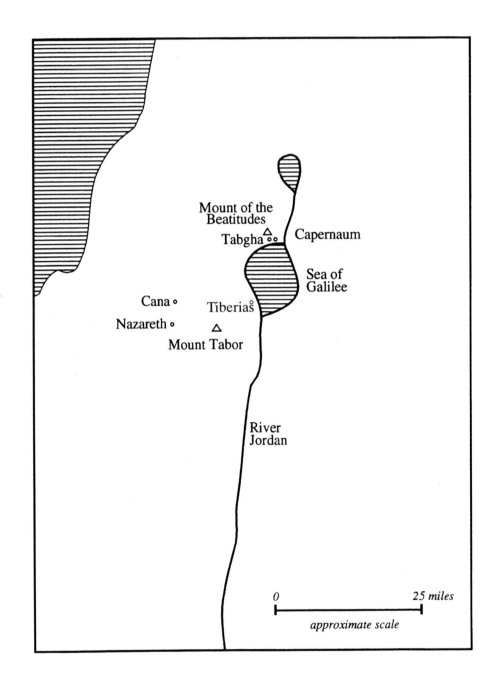

Mount of the
Beatitudes

Tabgha

Capernaum

Sea of
Galilee

Cana

Tiberias

Nazareth

Mount Tabor

River
Jordan

0   25 miles

approximate scale

1

Like a Painting and We Were Part of It

THE SEA OF GALILEE

Visiting the Sea of Galilee is one of the most outstanding memories of any pilgrimage to the Holy Land. This is because it has changed so little since the time of Jesus and also because so many events in Our Lord's life took place around its shores.

Thora was very excited about her own trip on the water which was planned for the day of her eighty-third birthday. So many of the stories she had heard in church and sung about in hymns were rooted near this place. The Sea of Galilee is only 11 kilometres wide and 21 kilometres long but its depth reaches 45 metres in parts. It is 'living water' and is therefore piped to various other dry parts of the region to help with irrigation and development of water supplies. It is mentioned in the Old Testament (Numbers 34:11; Joshua 13:27) and the villages and towns around the Sea form the backdrop for the first two years of Jesus' ministry.

Most pilgrim groups stay in or near to the town of Tiberias. The number of hotels in the resort has increased since the early 1980s. Many believe that the tall hotel blocks have spoilt the peace and ambience of the Tiberias region. From here pilgrims can take their boats to a variety of sites across the other side of the lake. One of the most popular destinations is the kibbutz En Gev which is close to many of the Christian churches. The boat trip takes about one hour. As you sail, you can reflect and ponder over Jesus' many works here. Usually the guide asks the captain of the boat to turn off the engines. This allows pilgrim groups to pray and read, to share in Holy Communion or just to meditate. It is a wonderful experience: you are back in the time of Jesus. Dame Thora crossed the lake ahead of her party so that she could be there, at the other side, to greet her pilgrims. It was to be a birthday she would never forget.

Reading
With the coming of evening that same day, Jesus said to them, 'Let us cross over to the other side.' And leaving the crowd behind they took him, just as he was, in the boat; and there were other boats with him. Then it began to blow a great

gale and the waves were breaking into the boat so that it was almost swamped. But he was in the stern, his head on a cushion, asleep. They woke him and said to him, 'Master, do you not care? We are lost!' And he woke up and rebuked the wind and said to the sea, 'Quiet now! Be calm!' And the wind dropped, and there followed a great calm. Then he said to them, 'Why are you so frightened? Have you still no faith?' They were overcome with awe and said to one another, 'Who can this be? Even the wind and the sea obey him.' (Mark 4:35–41)

Dame Thora reflects

❝I celebrated my eighty-third birthday on the Sea of Galilee. A few weeks after, someone said to me, 'Oh, you have had a birthday, haven't you? Where did you celebrate it – in London or at your country place?' I said to them, 'No, I celebrated it where Jesus had his – and you can't do better than that, can you?' And of course it was to be my last birthday with Jimmy. What a place for him to say 'Happy Birthday' to me – where Jesus had his!

I have a great imagination. We had arrived at our hotel by the Sea of Galilee late at night and it was a lovely surprise to see the Sea the next morning at sunrise from our balcony window. I knew we were going on the water and I couldn't wait until the next day. The boats have been altered to look like boats from Jesus' time. Even the boatmen wear the same types of costume to make it look as if they are from the New Testament.

I felt a real sense of peace when I got on the boat. It was a lovely crossing and you looked across to Jordan, up at the Golan Heights, back at Syria. Amazing! The water is very blue and from time to time I even spotted some of the many fish that are in that living water. At a certain point the captain turned off the engines. I can't describe the peace and tranquillity that I felt at that moment: it was quite amazing. Even Jimmy, who didn't usually say such things, was telling someone about the boat trip a few days afterwards and he said, 'There isn't really a way of describing the feeling when that boat was at rest.' When Jesus was on the boat and the storm suddenly blew up, he says, 'Peace, be still'. And if the 'be still' was that tranquillity then it was something that so impressed me that I will never forget it. It wasn't just the stillness: there was nothing – no lapping of the water on the side of the boat. Nothing. It was like a painting and we were part of it.

Our boat was full of Germans and, of course, they had a German pastor. Now I don't speak a word of German, but when he got into the bow of the boat and started to read from his Bible, I knew that it was the story of the fishes and loaves. I don't know 'loaf' or 'fishes' in German but I knew it was that story. When he had finished he came and sat in front of me and put his arm on the back of the seat and said to me, 'And do you believe in Jesus Christ?' And I said, 'What a sad woman I would be if I didn't.' He raised his hand and, to my great surprise, the entire German party sang 'Happy Birthday to You', in perfect English, on board that boat there on the Sea of Galilee. What a moment it was! This is one place that has not changed at all. It can't. It was a beautiful time.

The boat eventually arrived at its destination. Now the Jewish race are the smartest business community in the world. When you get off the boat there is a very nice coffee house near the wharf. I was really ready for a coffee by then – mid-morning and all that. The owner was talking to our guide, who told him that it was my birthday. I don't know what he said in Hebrew (the language of the Old Testament, which, by the way, is a lovely language with some amazing sounds) but the owner said something to me – 'Shalosh, mishet machin' or something. Then he said something to a little boy near him, by clipping him on the side of the head, and this beautiful child darted off. I thought that he was being told off but he came back a few minutes later with a lovely brooch for me. It's the size of a small biscuit but it is made of small shells from the bottom of the Sea of Galilee and they have all been painted in delicate little shades. It is beautiful. In English, he said, 'Happy Birthday'. Such kindness. I can't tell you. **"**

Our Hymn

"This is a lovely hymn to sing on the boat, particularly the second line of the first verse – 'Forgive our foolish ways'. That is something we should ask God every night. I certainly do. To sing the hymn in Galilee where it all happened is really thrilling. The 'sabbath rest by Galilee' is the calm that I could not describe. The whole hymn, written by a Quaker, is based on a poem.

I also prayed for peace in the world as we sang it. The Sea of Galilee is the meeting point of several countries and I was aware of that. I did not get bogged down in the politics of it; I just hope that people will learn peace and live together in love. I often imagine God, at the end of the day, putting on his bed slippers and saying, 'Well, the end of another day. Some of it has gone well and some of it has not been so good.' We come to him in honesty. **"**

Dear Lord and Father of mankind,
Forgive our foolish ways!
Reclothe us in our rightful mind,
In purer lives thy service find,
In deeper reverence praise.

In simple trust like theirs who heard,
Beside the Syrian sea,
The gracious calling of the Lord,
Let us, like them, without a word
Rise up and follow thee.

O sabbath rest by Galilee!
O calm of hills above,
Where Jesus knelt to share with thee
The silence of eternity,
Interpreted by love!

Drop thy still dews of quietness,
Till all our strivings cease;
Take from our souls the strain and stress,
And let our ordered lives confess
The beauty of thy peace.

Breathe through the heats of our desire
Thy coolness and thy balm;
Let sense be dumb, let flesh retire;
Speak through the earthquake, wind and fire,
O still small voice of calm!

(John Whittier, 1807–92)

Prayer
Lord Jesus Christ,
who commanded the wind and the waves to be still;
grant, in peace in our lives and joy in our hearts,
that we may have faith and confidence in you;
help us to encourage others to live lives of faith and hope;
this we ask in and through your holy name,
Amen.

A Birthday Prayer
Heavenly Father,
thank you for this, my birthday;
for the happy memories of birthdays past;
for my parents and family;
for the years you have given me and the time I have left to
    serve you here on earth.
Grant me happiness and love, so that I may share it with
    others.
Amen.

Peace in the World
Almighty God,
who created the heavens and the earth so that love could
    reign supreme.
We pray for peace in the world – for an end to war, hatred,
    violence and terrorism.
And we pray for the peace of God in people's hearts – that
    peace which passes all understanding.
Through Christ our Lord, the Prince of Peace,
Amen.

2

Followed Me Everywhere I Went

TABGHA – THE LOAVES
AND FISHES

The site commemorating the place where Jesus used the five loaves and two fishes to feed a multitude of people is one of the most striking of any pilgrimage. Today it is known as Tabgha, which means 'seven springs' in Arabic. It was here, according to tradition, that Jesus performed the miracle of the feeding of the five thousand at the place of the seven springs.

There have been several churches on this site. The present one was built in 1982 by the 'German Association in the Holy Land'. Apart from the church there is a small audio-visual centre which explains the work carried out there and an excellent bookshop with a range of gifts. The modern church is Byzantine in style and has a feeling of simplicity. In recent years it has become a favourite site for Jewish immigrants from former Soviet countries who joyously play their violins or violas in the hope of earning a few shekels.

The mosaics in the church depict the flowers and birds of the region. But your heart will be lifted as you approach the sanctuary and see the famous mosaic of the loaves and fishes. It is a wonderful spot to pray in; thankfully, guides are not allowed to speak inside. Thora decided to light her first Holy Land candle in this place.

Tabgha – the site commemorating the feeding of the five thousand

Reading

The apostles rejoined Jesus and told him all they had done and taught, and he said to them, 'Come away to some lonely place all by yourselves and rest for a while; for there were so many coming and going that there was no time even for them to eat. So they went off in the boat to a lonely place where they could be by themselves. But people saw them going, and many recognised them; and from every town they all hurried to the place on foot and reached it before them. So as he stepped ashore he saw a large crowd; and he took pity on them because they were like sheep without a shepherd, and he set himself to teach them at some length. By now it was getting very late, and his disciples came up to him and said, 'This is a lonely place and it is getting very late, so send them away and they can go to the farms and villages round about to buy themselves something to eat. He replied, 'Give them something to eat yourselves.' They answered, 'Are we to go and spend two hundred denarii on bread for them to eat?' He asked: 'How many loaves have you? Go and see.' And when they had found out they said, 'Five, and two fish.' Then he ordered them to get all the people to sit down in groups on the green grass and they sat down on the ground in squares of hundreds and fifties. Then he took the five loaves and the two fish, raised his eyes to heaven and said the blessing; then he broke the loaves and began handing them to his disciples to distribute among the people. He also shared out the two fish among them all. They all ate as much as they wanted. They collected twelve basketfuls of scraps of bread and pieces of fish. Those who had eaten the loaves numbered five thousand men. (Mark 6:30–44)

Dame Thora reflects

❝This is a lovely church and a special place. I am not sure

about the posh name that it is known by [Tabgha] but I will always remember that mosaic of the loaves and fishes. It's in the sanctuary of the simple and yet lovely church on the lakeside. It was one of the few things that I brought back for myself to look at – a double tile with the fishes and loaves of the mosaic on it and I have put that in my little cottage.

I lit a candle that day in the church. It seemed to follow me everywhere that I went. I didn't forget it and whenever I saw that mosaic in other shops it was with me.

As an actress I suppose I have a certain amount of imagination and that imagination gave me a lot of pleasure. I remembered Jesus in the upper room with the bread and wine when I thought about him feeding the five thousand here.

The Lord's Supper is a reminder of God's blessing to us every day. When I go to church in our village near Chichester I enjoy taking Communion and I can always see that famous painting of the Last Supper in my mind: the disciples gathered with Jesus around the table. I also see a picture of Jesus washing the feet of his disciples. Those words – 'This is my body. This is my blood.' – spoken when they were to Jesus' friends are very sad if you stop to think about them. Holy Communion is one form of actually getting on your knees and showing love and respect to God. It is a shame that it has also been the cause of so much division amongst the churches.

Making the loaves and fishes feed so many is a marvellous sign of Jesus' authority. You can imagine people saying today, 'You what? He's not Paul Daniels!' You have to believe in Jesus first before you can really understand. The feeding of the five thousand is a story left to us in print to help us believe. There must be hundreds of other similar stories that we simply do not know about. **"**

Our Hymn

"We had this very often on 'Praise Be!' It's a lovely hymn that can be sung to several tunes. We can all be selfish in religion and there is a danger that the more religious you become the more selfish you are. We have to keep our eyes open to how other people see us. 'Alleluia! Sing to Jesus!' is a wonderful hymn of praise that keeps us focused on God. **"**

> Alleluia! Sing to Jesus!
> His the sceptre, his the throne;
> Alleluia! His the triumph,
> His the victory alone:
> Hark! The songs of peaceful Sion
> Thunder like a mighty flood;
> Jesus out of every nation
> Hath redeemed us by his blood.
>
> Alleluia! Not as orphans
> Are we left in sorrow now;
> Alleluia! He is near us,
> Faith believes, nor questions how:
> Though the cloud from sight received him,
> When the forty days were o'er,
> Shall our hearts forget his promise,
> 'I am with you evermore'.
>
> Alleluia! Bread of Angels,
> Thou on earth our food, our stay;

Alleluia! Here the sinful
Flee to Thee from day to day:
Intercessor, Friend of sinners,
Earth's redeemer, plead for me,
Where the songs of all the sinless
Sweep across the crystal sea.

Alleluia! King eternal,
Thee the Lord of Lords we own;
Alleluia! Born of Mary,
Earth thy footstool, heaven thy throne:
Thou within the veil hast entered,
Robed in flesh our great high priest;
Thou on earth both priest and victim
In the Eucharistic feast.

(W. Chatterton Dix, 1837–98)

Prayer
We do not presume to come to this thy table, O Merciful
Lord, trusting in our own righteousness, but in thy manifold
and great mercies. We are not worthy so much as to gather
up the crumbs under thy table. But thou art the same Lord,
whose nature is always to have mercy: Grant us therefore,
gracious Lord, so to eat the flesh of thy dear Son Jesus
Christ, and to drink his blood, that we may evermore dwell
in him, and he in us. Amen.

(*The Alternative Service Book, Rite B*)

3

None of This Had Altered

THE MOUNT OF THE BEATITUDES

This site is the highlight for many people in the Galilee part of the pilgrimage. The church has been constructed from the local basalt rock and the arches are made from the white stone of Nazareth. The hill – called by many 'a natural amphitheatre' – is accepted as the one Jesus climbed to deliver his famous Sermon on the Mount (recorded in Matthew chapters 5–7). There are eight sides to the church, reflecting eight of the beatitudes, and the dome itself represents the ninth saying of Jesus, in which he talks about persecution.

There are marvellous views of the Sea of Galilee, some wonderful gardens where open-air services are held, and a simple gift shop for postcards and beads. The freshly squeezed orange juice in the coach park is excellent! When Dame Thora's double-decker bus arrived there was great expectation amongst other British groups. I think that we encountered the most 'Last of the Summer Wine' fans here. Thora was to read in the Holy Land for the first time. She was as excited as they were.

Reading
Seeing the crowds, Jesus went on to the mountain. And when he was seated his disciples came to him. Then he began to speak. This is what he taught them:

How blessed are the poor in spirit:
the Kingdom of Heaven is theirs.
Blessed are the gentle:
they shall have the earth as inheritance.
Blessed are those who mourn:
they shall be comforted.
Blessed are those who hunger and thirst for righteousness:
they shall have their fill.
Blessed are the merciful:
they shall have mercy shown to them.
Blessed are the pure in heart:
they shall see God.
Blessed are the peacemakers:
they shall be recognised as children of God.
Blessed are those who are persecuted in the cause of
    uprightness:
the Kingdom of Heaven is theirs.
                                    (Matthew 5:1–10)

Dame Thora reflects

"This is where I first read from the Bible on my pilgrimage and I won't forget it. The reading above, from the Gospel of Matthew, speaks for itself, but I found it very moving to read it there. It was like a tiny glen. We sat on the slopes and Jan and I read the story of the blessed. There were beautiful trees and flowers – the green, the beauty. All the grass and the wildlife were so lovely and they were all still. We were not being particularly religious as we read Jesus' sayings but I remember thinking there, 'What a lot people miss out on who do not have a religion.'

When I was looking across the hills of Galilee I remembered how many small stories there are in the New Testament which start 'He went up into the hills', or 'They went up into the hills'. I had no trouble at all in thinking that none of this had altered and then I remembered how much I had enjoyed walking when I was younger. I was a great walker. I can't walk so much now – but then I can't tap dance either! If someone had said, 'Well, there's this chap from over the hills, you should come and hear him speak', then people would go. We do it now.

I'd also like to say something about the nuns and monks we saw all over the Holy Land. What wonderful people they are! They do marvellous things to help us feel welcome, many of them giving up much that we take for granted. When I saw the Sisters working so hard at the Church on the Mount of Beatitudes I prayed for my own friends who are nuns or monks. I once went to do a 'Praise Be!' programme in Norfolk. Most people expect the Reverend Mother to be called Martha or Matilda, but – and I don't know why I say this – you don't expect it to be Pamela, do you? Forty some-

The Church on the Mount of the Beatitudes

thing, nylon stockings and caring for everyone. We had done a recording in the convent.

When it came to saying goodbye, the director and the crew all gathered to say 'thank you very much'. Pamela bent down to kiss me and as the director started to slide the door of the van to, I saw her fingers in the door. That dear little sweet hand as it was hit by the door. And I saw the tears spring to her eyes as she had her hand trapped – I saw that. I was out of that van quicker than I have told you this and I put my arms around her and said, 'Oh Mother Pamela, I am so sorry.' She insisted she would be OK and she fought back any tears.

Well, of course, the wrong thing – I hated the director who had closed the door from that moment onwards for the rest of the journey. He kept saying, 'I'm really sorry, I didn't know that her hand was in the door.' Well, the whole crew stayed at a motel for the night and it was freezing cold. I got everything out of my case to keep me warm. I got into bed, but I couldn't sleep straight away so I started to say my prayers and I said, 'Dear Lord, don't let that poor little sister's fingers be blue or anything. Don't let her suffer because she is doing such marvellous work for you.' I woke up quite early the next morning and I thought again about the accident the day before. It was about 6.30 am. I prayed for Pamela again.

During the day I got to a phone three times and each time she was at prayer or a service or whatever. In fact I didn't actually manage to speak to her until two days later. I asked her how she was and she told me that her fingers were OK, just a little bruised as you'd expect. But then she said, 'Forgive me asking you, dear Thora, but did you pray for me?' And I said, 'Yes, I did', and

I explained about how cold I had been and how I'd prayed for her. 'Oh, I know when it was that night, and the following morning,' she said so confidently. She is a remarkable person.

I loved seeing the monks and the nuns from all over the world. Whether in Jerusalem or in the desert or in Galilee, there they all were. And on the Mount of Beatitudes the French sisters had a lovely smile. And what a wonderful view over the Sea of Galilee as you approached the Mount. **"**

Our Hymn

"This is a good old hymn from Sunday School days and one I always enjoy singing. The words are so true to the feeling you have when you are at Beatitudes. **"**

> Blest are the pure in heart,
> For they shall see our God;
> The secret of the Lord is theirs,
> Their soul is Christ's abode.
>
> The Lord, who left the heavens
> Our life and peace to bring,
> To dwell in lowliness with men,
> Their pattern and their king;
>
> Still to the lowly soul
> He doth himself impart,
> And for his dwelling and his throne
> Chooseth the pure in heart.
>
> Lord, we thy presence seek;
> May ours this blessing be;

Give us a pure and lowly heart,
A temple meet for thee.

(J. Keble and others)

Prayer

Almighty God, we thank you for sending your Son, our Saviour Jesus Christ, into the world to teach us the Good News of your Kingdom. Help us to hear his words, to understand the challenge and then to seek your grace in living out the Kingdom in our own lives so that others may be brought to a knowledge of your new and living way, through Jesus Christ our Lord, Amen.

4

What Do You Think I Am Doing Here?

CAPERNAUM, THE TOWN
OF JESUS

The heat was quite intense when we arrived at Capernaum (Capharnaum). The thermometer on the coach registered 97°F. Thora and Scottie were unperturbed. It is about 500 metres from the coach park to the gatehouse marking the site of the old town. There is a small charge for entry which helps the Franciscans to maintain the site. The Brothers have been there since 1894 and they have developed the site.

Archaeologists have discovered extensive ruins dating back to the time of Jesus and even to the second century BC. The reconstructed synagogue reveals how wealthy some of the inhabitants must have been for it is not built of the local basalt rock but of limestone, probably from the Jerusalem region. There are many ruins of houses and shops to see and amongst them probably those of the home of Peter the Apostle. During the 1980s controversial planning proposals were passed, allowing the building of a very modern Roman Catholic church over the ruins. You have to judge the results for yourself.

Thora was aware that there are so many events and incidents associated with Capernaum in the Gospels and later that evening she looked some of them up in the Bible. Here is just one of them.

Reading

They went as far as Capernaum, and at once on the sabbath he went into the synagogue and began to teach. And his teaching made a deep impression on them because, unlike the scribes, he taught them with authority. And at once in their synagogue there was a man with an unclean spirit, and it shouted, 'What do you want with us, Jesus of Nazareth? Have you come to destroy us? I know who you are, the Holy One of God!' but Jesus rebuked it saying, 'Be quiet! Come out of him!' And the unclean spirit threw the man into convulsions and with a loud cry went out of him. The people were so astonished that they started asking one another what it all meant, saying, 'Here is a teaching that is new, and with authority behind it: he gives orders even to unclean spirits and they obey him.' And his reputation at once spread everywhere, through all the surrounding Galilean countryside. (Mark 1:21–28)

Dame Thora reflects

"As you approach Capernaum the views are wonderful, I really can't tell you. It was very hot and there were some lovely flowers all along the road.

When our coach arrived it was one of more than about twenty and there were quite a few British groups amongst them. Word soon got around that Thora was in Capernaum! My goodness, it was like being back at home. You feel very flattered. I was grateful that I was there for people to say, 'Hello, Thora. What are you doing here?' I mean you feel like saying, 'What do you think I am doing here?' This is where Jesus spent a good deal of his time.

We were praising the Lord, but we were doing it simply by being there and drinking in the atmosphere. Don't forget that this was Jesus' favourite town. Everyone in Nazareth knew Jesus as the son of Mary and Joseph. He had been to school there, had his mates there, everyone knew him. It wouldn't have been easy for him to teach those people about the Kingdom of God. So Jesus set off towards the Sea from just a few miles away and it was this small town of Capernaum that he found most welcoming and which he came back to time and time again.

Although there is no one living there today, you really get the feeling that this was the town of Jesus. It was here that he stayed often, taught in the synagogue, chatted to people in their homes and in the streets. The other thing I remember about Capernaum is the flowers, plants and trees. They were beautiful – as if they were growing especially for Jesus. I remember at my Wesleyan Sunday School – we didn't get a lot of tracts but those that we did get we would keep in our Bibles – and I had one of Jesus amongst the flowers and it said 'the Gardener'.

What a lovely description: Jesus amongst those colourful
plants and flowers. **99**

Our Hymn

66 'The Kingdom of God' is one of those special phrases
that it is hard to explain to people but I think we all
have our own idea of what it means to us. However
you find God, in whatever way you discover him, you
should go and seek the Kingdom first. We sang this
hymn in 'a round' – one side singing it, followed by the
other when the first reached 'Alleluia'. **99**

> Seek ye first the kingdom of God,
> And his righteousness,
> And all these things shall be added unto you,
> Alleluia, Alleluia.
>
> Man shall not live by bread alone,
> But by every word,
> That proceeds from the mouth of God,
> Alleluia, Alleluia.
>
> Ask and it shall be given unto you,
> Seek and ye shall find,
> Knock and the door shall be opened up to you,
> Alleluia, Alleluia.

(Karen Lafferty)

Prayer

The grace of our Lord Jesus Christ, the love of God and the
fellowship of the Holy Spirit, be amongst you and remain
with you always, Amen.

5

A Good View from up There

MOUNT TABOR – THE TRANSFIGURATION OF JESUS

My own devotion to the Transfiguration of Jesus is well attested elsewhere, namely in a book which was published on the same day that our party visited Mount Tabor. Dame Thora had kindly agreed to launch the book, *The*

Transfiguration of Jesus, on the mountain itself. It was to be a day we would not forget.

Mount Tabor is one of two sites which tradition suggests was the place of the Transfiguration: Mount Hermon is the other. The mountain is approached through the Arab village of Dabburiya and you have to leave your coach to take a Mercedes taxi up to the summit. It was hardly the way Jesus travelled! At the top of the mountain the taxis leave you at the entrance to a courtyard where the Franciscan community has built an attractive retreat house. There is also a small gift shop here. The church itself is quite beautiful; it is built on a site where a church has stood since 422. There is also an Orthodox Church of Elijah where three monks currently live.

The Franciscan Brothers kindly allowed us to launch the book in the church itself. We gathered to hear Thora confess that this was a story that she had hardly come across in her own faith. She said that the Transfiguration was something we all ought to know more about. We heard the story and prayed for God's Transfiguration blessing on each of us.

Reading

Six days later, Jesus took with him Peter and James and John and led them up a high mountain on their own by themselves. There in their presence he was transfigured: his clothes became brilliantly white, whiter than any earthly bleacher could make them. Elijah appeared to them with Moses; and they were talking to Jesus. Then Peter spoke to Jesus, 'Rabbi', he said, 'it is wonderful for us to be here; so let us make three shelters, one for you, one for Moses and one for Elijah.' He did not know what to say; they were so frightened. And a cloud came, covering them in shadow; and from the cloud there came a voice, 'This is my Son, the Beloved. Listen to him.' Then suddenly, when they looked round, they saw no one with them any more but only Jesus. (Mark 9:2–8)

Dame Thora reflects

"This was one of the highlights for me. We went up the mountain by car because the coach can't manage those hairpin bends. I wish I could have walked but I couldn't. So the taxis took us on a fantastic journey. As the car went round the bends I thought of Jesus with Peter, James and John plodding up this mountain. And when you don't know about a story and then realise what it meant for Jesus it is inspiring. It really was a discovery: I came across the Transfiguration story for the first time.

When I was talking to Brother Andrew, one of the Franciscan Brothers on the top of the mountain (or should I say, when he was talking to me because I listened most of the time – me being a woman and an actress on top of that!) I listened to this lovely man as Brother Andrew spoke to me. It didn't matter what kind of simple things I asked; it was as though he'd expected me to ask these things. And he said to me, 'Will you take a happy memory of this place back with you to London?' I assured him that it would be more than that: 'Don't think that I'm silly, but every time I put my foot on to the ground on this mountain I wonder if Jesus had his foot just there.' And his reply was marvellous: 'If that's where you put your feet, that is where he put his.' I have remembered that.

The service we had in the church was truly wonderful. We praised God together and young Domenico (in that fetching Italian accent) read from the Bible. As Peter himself says, 'It's good Lord to be here'! The backdrop in the church was also out of this world – Jesus with

Dame Thora and Rob Marshall, launching *The Transfiguration of Jesus* on Mount Tabor

Moses and Elijah in mosaics above our heads. There was no feeling at all that this was not the right place. Everyone really enjoyed Mount Tabor and there was a deep feeling of respect and reverence for this place.

But I had never understood the Transfiguration before this trip. It really came to life for me. If you have been brought up in the Church you still might not know about this marvellous story. Finding out about the Transfiguration was one of the greatest things that ever happened to me in my life. I have spoken to people since – many actors and actresses who have a real faith of their own as good Christians – and talked about the Transfiguration, saying that I hadn't understood what it was all about. And they too say, 'Well, tell us about it. What happened there?' It is worth going to the Holy Land just to find out about this story. Jesus had a good view from up there. He could see everything very clearly and God was with him. And the glory shone out.

There was a cross that I loved in the gift shop. I like to wear a cross – not to say 'Look, I'm a Christian' but because it gives me a great deal of comfort. But I gave this cross to Brother Andrew and he blessed it all the way through the time that we were talking. So you might guess I love that cross very dearly. **"**

Our Hymn
"Now this is one of those hymns which defies anyone who says that modern hymns can't be wonderful. It fits the Transfiguration so well. It is absolutely *for* there. 'Be still, for the presence of the Lord, the Holy One, is here' calls us to that stillness which is so special and which you have to experience in the Holy Land for yourself. **"**

Be still, for the presence of the Lord, the Holy One, is here.
Come, bow before Him now, with reverence and fear.
In Him no sin is found, we stand on holy ground.
Be still, for the Spirit of the Lord, the Holy One, is here.

Be still, for the glory of the Lord is shining all around;
He burns with holy fire, with splendour he is crowned.
How awesome is the sight, our radiant King of light!
Be still, for the glory of the Lord is shining all around.

Be still, for the power of the Lord is moving in this place,
He comes to cleanse and heal, to minister his grace.
No work too hard for him, in faith receive from Him;
Be still, for the power of the Lord is moving in this place.

(David J. Evans)

From an American Priest
To the world as to his disciples, Jesus was
Revealed as an ordinary man. It was deeds
And words which took them by surprise and
Negated ordinariness. Only on this lofty-sited
Single occasion was there a visual, startling
Fundamental Nature perceived. It was as
If His sumation of the Law and Prophets
Grew from speech into reality seen and
Understood – if only for a moment. Then the
Radiant vision of singularity receded in
A cloud of mist. And even as that brief and
Tantalizing image was grasped for – lest
It be lost – there followed awesome words.
Oh disciples of today: regard neither light
Nor cloud. Hear Him in heart, in mind and soul!

Prayer

Almighty and everlasting God, whose blessed Son revealed himself to his chosen apostles when he was transfigured on the holy mount, and amidst the excellent glory spake with Moses and Elijah of his death which he would accomplish at Jerusalem: grant to us thy servants, that beholding the brightness of thy countenance, we may be strengthened to bear the cross, through the same Jesus Christ our Lord. Amen.

(Scottish Prayer Book)

6

I Wanted To Weep, I Don't Know Why

NAZARETH

Dame Thora was very keen to visit Nazareth. She had read about it but wanted to see the town with her own eyes. Nazareth is one of the most appealing and amiable towns in the Holy Land. The visitor immediately has the impression that it has managed to avoid scenes of great war, brutality and bloodshed over the years. The Arabs who live here are of a generally peaceful nature and they are known locally as 'Israeli Arabs'. Because it is a Christian and Muslim town, many Jews come here on Saturdays to do their shopping when shops in the Jewish towns are closed. It would seem that everyone is welcome in Nazareth.

Nazareth is the place where Mary was born and brought up. It was here that the Annunciation took place. And it was in Nazareth that Jesus spent the majority of his years, carefully preparing himself for the ministry that was to lie ahead of him. The modern Church of the Annunication has always made an impression on me, for two obvious reasons. The first is the way in which the present church has been built over the cave of the Annunciation, which was designated as the site in the second century and has been preserved from that time. It is one of the most sacred sites for Christians in the Holy Land. But another marvellous feature of the new church is the series of sculptures of the Madonna and Child which have been provided by countries from all over the world, each in their own native local materials. Leon, our guide, pointed us in the direction of the Japanese Madonna, which particularly stands out because the sleeve of Mary is made from pure mother-of-pearl.

The coach arrived in the busy market town. We made our way up to the church through streets crowded with a range of stalls selling everything from plastic dolls and wooden cribs to shoes, spices and coathangers. It was, said Thora, 'any other town and yet it wasn't'.

Reading
In the sixth month the angel Gabriel was sent by God to a town in Galilee called Nazareth, to a virgin betrothed to

a man named Joseph, of the House of David; and the virgin's name was Mary. He went in and said to her, 'Rejoice, you who enjoy God's favour! The Lord is with you.' She was deeply disturbed by these words and asked herself what greeting this could mean, but the angel said to her, 'Mary do not be afraid; you have won God's favour. Look! You are to conceive in your womb and bear a son and you must name him Jesus. He will be great and will be called the Son of the Most High. The Lord God will give him the throne of his ancestor David; he will rule over the House of Jacob for ever and his reign will have no end. Mary said to the angel, 'But how can this come about, since I have no knowledge of this man?' The angel answered, 'The Holy Spirit will come upon you, and the power of the Most High will cover you with its shadow. And so the child will be holy and will be called the Son of God.' (Luke 1:26–36)

Dame Thora reflects

❝It was a real town, Nazareth. Busy, with traffic, lots of people and a happy market where they were selling everything from shoes to soap. When I actually saw the town sign saying 'Welcome to Nazareth' I wanted to weep, I don't know why. It was written, like all the road signs, in Hebrew, Arabic and English. We were here, in the town of Mary and Joseph. We were in the place where Jesus had grown up as a child.

I remember looking at Nazareth and thinking – 'well it could be anywhere!' But then, no, it couldn't. The hills around Nazareth and the mountains were very impressive and I am sure that it has not altered very much at all. My understudy in the theatre, Connie Merrygold, had a schoolteacher friend who always seemed to have a lovely story to tell about a child. One

day he asked them to draw something that wasn't Jesus
with sheep, or Jesus surrounded by people. Remember, Jesus lived an ordinary life in an ordinary town –
Nazareth. So one little boy drew a shop and above the
shop he wrote the sign 'J. Christ, Carpenter'.

After we left the main building of the Annunciation
church we crossed a lovely courtyard under which there
are even more excavations. This leads, eventually, to the
Church of St Jospeh. I also loved this church. Joseph
was a wonderful man. Whenever he is portrayed – on
paintings, cards or even in a model of a crib – he always
has a sweet face. He was happy to stay in the background and let God get on with it. I suppose my Scottie
knew a bit what it must have been like for Joseph; I'm
the one that people always talked to and latched on to
and Jimmy just walked alongside, usually with a smile
on his face. God bless him!   **"**

Our Hymn
"This was often requested on 'Praise Be!'. Of course, we
couldn't always play the hymns that were requested but
we did play this one. It is the setting to music of Mary's
song, using modern words, and it's a good one.

Having been married to a musician, and all my family
being musical, I must say that there is a lot of music of
today which is fresh and exciting. A lot of young people
come to church because the music has become much
more modern in recent years. As long as God is being
praised we should be happy. And so this modern trans-
lation of Mary – it's a lovely song of praise.   **"**

Tell out, my soul, the greatness of the Lord:
unnumbered blessings, give my spirit voice;

73

An aerial view of Nazareth

Tender to them the promise of his word;
in God my Saviour shall my heart rejoice.

Tell out my soul, the greatness of his name:
make known his might, the deeds his arm has done;
His mercy sure, from age to age the same;
his holy name, the Lord, the mighty one.

Tell out, my soul, the greatness of his might:
powers and dominions lay their glory by;
Proud hearts and stubborn wills are put to flight,
the hungry fed, the humble lifted high.

Tell out, my soul, the glories of his word:
firm is his promise, and his mercy sure.
Tell out, my soul, the greatness of the Lord
to children's children and for evermore.

(Timothy Dudley-Smith, b. 1926)

Prayers
Hail Mary, full of Grace, the Lord is with thee,
Blessed art thou among women and blessed is the fruit of
    thy womb, Jesus.
Holy Mary, Mother of God, pray for us sinners now and
    at the hour of our death.
Amen.

My soul doth magnify the Lord: and my spirit hath rejoiced
    in God my Saviour.
For he hath regarded: the lowliness of his handmaiden.
For behold, from henceforth: all generations shall call me
    blessed.

For he that is mighty hath magnified me: and holy is his
Name.

And his mercy is on them that fear him: throughout all
generations.

He hath shewn strength with his arm: he hath scattered the
proud in the imagination of their hearts.

He hath put down the mighty from their seat: and hath
exalted the humble and meek.

He hath filled the hungry with good things: and the rich
he hath sent empty away.

He remembering his mercy hath holpen his servant Israel:
as he promised to our forefathers, Abraham and his
seed, for ever.

(Book of Common Prayer)

7

All the Brides Who Had Walked Down Here

CANA IN GALILEE

Cana is just a few kilometres from Nazareth. It is more or less a suburb of Nazareth now, but in the time of Jesus it would have been a distinct village community in its own right. Its 13,000 inhabitants today are Christians and Muslims. About 4,000 young people attend schools and colleges in this town. They are a very friendly people.

When we arrived in Cana, Dame Thora was very excited. Although the churches are a good walk from where the bus dropped us, Thora was unperturbed. 'I want to see the wedding church,' she said. It was here that Jesus came from Nazareth to perform the miracle that was the first sign of his messiahship. It was to be a wonderful occasion for all those who witnessed his act. We visited the Franciscan church which tradition suggests stands on the exact site of the miracle. Nearby there is an Orthodox church which has two very old water storage jars like the one held by the Franciscans.

Cana is now famous with pilgrims for two main reasons. It is a place of thanksgiving for the sacrament of marriage: many thousands of people renew their marriage vows here. (It is also a place where hundreds of Christian couples are married every year.) But it is also famous for its wine – Cana wine. Here you can buy a bottle for your own church for that special Holy Communion Service on Christmas Eve or for a friend's wedding.

Reading

On the third day there was a wedding at Cana in Galilee. The mother of Jesus was there, and Jesus and his disciples had also been invited. And they ran out of wine, since the wine provided for the feast had all been used, and the mother of Jesus said to them, 'They have no wine.' Jesus said, 'Woman, what do you want from me? My hour has not yet come.' His mother said to his servants, 'Do whatever he tells you.' There were six stone jars standing there, meant for the ablutions that are customary among the Jews: each could hold twenty or thirty gallons. Jesus said to the servants, 'Fill the jars with water,' and they filled them to the brim. Then he said to them, 'Draw some out now and take it to the president of the feast.' They did this; the president tasted the water now become wine. Having no idea where it came from – though the servants who had drawn it knew – the president of the feast called the bridegroom and said, 'Everyone serves good wine first and the worse wine when the guests are well wined; but you have kept the best wine till now.' This was the first of Jesus' signs: it was at Cana in Galilee. (John 2:1–11)

Dame Thora reflects

❝Cana is not far away from Nazareth. I was very happy to see that Mary and Jesus did not have too far to walk from Nazareth to Cana for the wedding feast. It was about eight minutes by bus. In fact, we'd only just got back on our double-decker when we had to get off it again! That was after Spartacus (the driver) managed to close the bus door on my foot – totally my own fault, mind you!

We walked from the bus down a little alley to a lovely church. As we stood in that tiny church I didn't waste a moment. I sat down and tried to visualise it all, and thought, 'Mary would have had to get ready for this wedding.' I was thinking of the practical things. She went with a couple of neighbours. And they always drank the good wine first.

I found myself looking at bits of floor and thinking of all the brides who had walked down here. It's one of the most popular churches in the world to get married in, and no wonder.

Wherever the feast was, you could see his mother saying to her son, 'There is no wine left. They have run out of wine!' There is always water. But Jesus was there and 'alleyup' – there is the wine. Jimmy and I were married for fifty-eight years. And we renewed our marriage vows together and got a wedding certificate from Cana in Galilee to prove it. It was lovely. I have it pinned up in my study. The Reverend Rob signed it. Quite a few other couples did the same. We'd all been to a wedding. I was very lucky in my marriage. When you have got the right one it's a blessing. I would never dare to criticise anyone who has been divorced. My daughter has been through that, though she is now happily married to William. And now I believe that it is nearly as wrong to stay with the wrong person within the intimacy of marriage as it is to separate. Marriage is not just a piece of paper. It is a gift. I was asked a few weeks ago to do a short talk on love. It was to be recorded and they agreed to bring the recording machine to my flat.

We sat down and I said to this nice young fella, 'It's a great subject but I could talk about it for an hour, because when you are a child you love your brother equally as much as you love your mother but it's a different type of love.' And that's just the start. You cannot describe all the different types of love. And the young fella said, 'Oh, wait a minute while I put the machine on.' I was already in full flow about love. I think one of the nicest things that people ever say to me – and forgive me for saying it – is that I give a lot of love away. I can only explain that by saying that it is because I have that much around me. And that is God's love. In order to love and be loved – you can't really describe it.

After the service in the church – where we heard a reading, sang a hymn, said some prayers and then renewed our marriage vows – we came back into the lovely warm air and into the courtyard. Just opposite the church there is a little shop where the man was giving each of our group a little thimbleful of wine to taste. Clever businessman, of course. Sell what else? They sold everything, I know, but the wine was the obvious thing. A lot of our group bought some souvenirs of this lovely little village; most bought at least one bottle of Cana wine for a future wedding or to use at a special Communion service back in their church at home. **99**

Our Hymn

66The hymn that we sang in the wedding church after we had all renewed our wedding vows was 'Love Divine' – and this was requested so often in the 'Praise Be!' letters that I used to receive by the sackful. People really love this hymn because it is about the love of God and also about the way we are to be to each other. **99**

> Love Divine, all loves excelling,
> Joy of heaven, to earth come down,
> Fix in us thy humble dwelling,
> All thy faithful mercies crown.
> Jesu, thou art all compassion,
> Pure unbounded love thou art;
> Visit us with thy salvation,
> Enter every trembling heart.
>
> Come, almighty to deliver,
> Let us all thy grace receive;
> Suddenly return, and never,
> Never more thy temples leave.
> Thee we would be always blessing,
> Serve thee as thy hosts above;

81

Pray, and praise thee, without ceasing,
Glory in thy perfect love.

Finish then thy new creation:
Pure and spotless let us be;
Let us see thy great salvation,
Perfectly restored in thee;
Changed from glory into glory,
Till in heaven we take our place,
Till we cast our crowns before thee,
Lost in wonder, love and praise.

(Charles Wesley, 1707–88)

Prayer
Eternal God, and Father of us all, we thank you for your creation of marriage. Bless all husbands and wives: may your presence enrich their lives and enable them to do your will. Help them to cherish each other in both good and bad times. Strengthen those who find marriage difficult, comfort those who are in despair and help all to share each other's burdens, for your sake. Amen.

(*Mothers' Union Service Book*, p. 39)

8

Thanking God for New Life

THE BAPTISM SITE

The River Jordan is an impressive river. It is 252 kilometres long and therefore by far the longest river in the Holy Land. It flows through the Sea of Galilee into the Dead Sea, though between the two its journey is dramatic and unpredictable. In the New Testament the River Jordan is most famous as the water in which John the Baptist baptised Jesus and other believers as a mark of their rebirth into the Christian faith (see Mark 1).

The fact that Jesus, according to tradition, is said to have been baptised somewhere between where the Allenby and Abdullah bridges cross the river today means that the traditional site has been in 'no man's land' between Israel and Jordan for much of the twentieth century. Because of this the Israelis have developed a special site just outside Tiberias where Christian pilgrims can assemble to remember the baptism of Jesus. Next to the coach and car park there is an excellent gift shop and a cafeteria. The River Jordan itself is approached via a series of stairs into the water. Here, Christians of all denominations can renew their baptismal vows and those wanting baptism can actually be baptised in the River Jordan. Called Yardenit, the site is one of my favourite spots, probably because it is a place of rest and reflection and no one pretends that this was the actual place. What we can be certain of is that this is the river.

Reading

It was at this time that Jesus came from Nazareth in Galilee and was baptised in the Jordan by John. And at once, as he was coming up out of the water, he saw the heavens torn apart and the Spirit, like a dove, descending on him. And a voice came from heaven, 'You are my Son, the Beloved; my favour rests on you.' (Mark 1:9–11)

Dame Thora reflects

"What a lovely place this was. We were ready for a coffee for one thing after more than an hour in our double-decker bus. Spartacus (the driver) opened the doors and

84

we all went the short walk to a kind of terrace. Now I can recommend the date honey here – it's the only place that you can buy it tasting quite so nice. And there are small water bottles which you buy and fill up with River Jordan water in case you know of someone whose baby is to be baptised. Fancy having a christening with real River Jordan water!

We then renewed the promises that either we had made or our Godparents had made for us at our baptism. A baptism is much more than giving a baby a name: it's about thanking God for new life and expressing a wish that God is involved in your life from the very start. And of course when Jesus came to the River Jordan he knew that all the preparation he had been involved in was coming to an end. Now the teaching and the miracles would start. His ministry was about to get under way. It really was a very important moment in Our Lord's life.

When God says, 'This is my beloved Son, in whom I am well pleased' in the Bible story, I am reminded of God's word on the top of the Mountain of the Transfiguration: 'This is my beloved Son. Listen to Him.' In both instances God speaks to us in a wonderful way. **"**

Our Hymn

"This hymn is sung to the same tune as 'Lord of all hopefulness' and is a lovely meditation on what it means to belong to Jesus. As you sing the words the idea of baptism as a kind of badge of Christianity comes to mind. It doesn't matter what denomination we are, only that God is our vision, 'O Ruler of all'. **"**

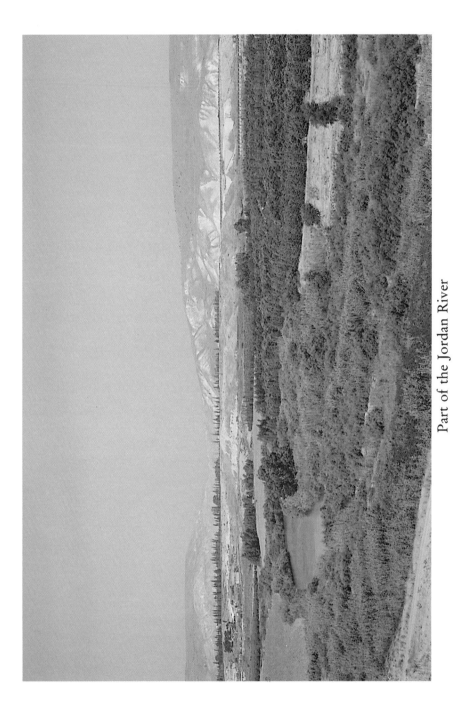

Part of the Jordan River

Be Thou my vision, O Lord of my heart;
Naught be all else to me, save that Thou art –
Thou my best thought, by day or by night,
Waking or sleeping, Thy presence my light.

Be Thou my wisdom, Thou my true Word;
I ever with Thee, Thou with me, Lord;
Thou my great Father, I Thy true son;
Thou in me dwelling and I with Thee one.

Riches I heed not, nor man's empty praise,
Thou mine inheritance, now and always:
Thou and Thou only, first in my heart,
High King of heaven, my treasure Thou art.

High King of heaven, after victory is won,
May I reach heaven's joys, O bright heaven's Sun!
Heart of my own heart, whatever befall,
Still be my vision, O Ruler of all.

(Ancient Irish, tr. Mary Elizabeth Byrne, 1880–1931)

Prayer
The Renewal of Baptismal Vows
Q: Do you believe and trust in God the Father, creator of
heaven and earth?
A: I believe and trust in God the Father who made me and
loves me.

Q: Do you believe and trust in his Son Jesus Christ, who
was transfigured, raised and ascended in glory?
A: I believe and trust in Jesus and pray that he may inspire
me.

Q: Do you believe and trust in his Holy Spirit who gives life to the Church today?

A: I believe and trust in the Holy Spirit who helps me to love God and my neighbour this day.

Make thyself manifest, O Lord, in this water and grant to him who is baptised in it so to be transformed, that he may put off the old man, which is corrupted by deceitful lusts, and may put on the new man, which is formed fresh according to the image of the Creator. Grafted through baptism into the likeness of thy death, may he become a partaker also in thy resurrection. May he guard the gift of thy Holy Spirit, may he increase the measure of grace which has been entrusted to him, and so may he receive the prize which is God's calling to life above, being numbered among the first born whose names are written in heaven.

(From the Eastern Orthodox Liturgy, Blessing of the baptismal font. *The Oxford Book of Prayer*, p. 215)

PART THREE

Towards the Holy City

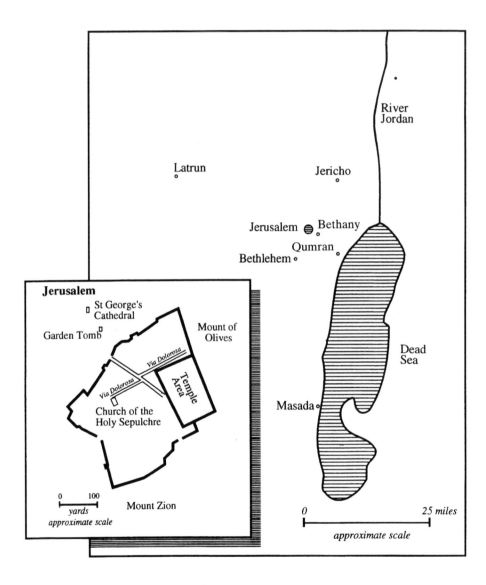

River
Jordan

Latrun
○

Jericho
○

Jerusalem ◉ Bethany
○
Qumran
○
Bethlehem ○

Dead
Sea

Masada ○

Jerusalem

□ St George's
Cathedral

Garden Tomb □

Mount of
Olives

Via Dolorosa

Via Dolorosa

Temple
Area

□ Church of the
Holy Sepulchre

0   100

yards
approximate scale

Mount Zion

0   25 *miles*

approximate scale

1

The Next Day in Marble Arch

FRUITS FROM THE DESERT

Travelling through the oasis around the town of Jericho and along the old West Bank road towards Tiberias, you can only sit and wonder at the achievements of modern irrigation techniques when it comes to what Israelis call 'pushing back the wilderness'. For what was once dry and barren is slowly becoming new land where flowers, vegetables and fruit are grown in great abundance.

Towards the Holy City

After his baptism in the River Jordan, Jesus went into the wilderness for forty days and forty nights. There he pondered over the future of his ministry and was at the mercy of the forces of evil. He was tempted yet he was without sin. Dame Thora's double-decker bus crossed much of this wilderness area. Near the excavations at Jericho it is possible to view the site alleged to be the Mount of Temptation where Our Saviour spent much of his time. It is a place for a moment of sober reflection on fasting and prayer.

Reading

Then Jesus was led by the Spirit out into the desert to be put to the test by the devil. He fasted for forty days and forty nights, after which he was hungry, and the tester came to him and said to him, 'If you are the Son of God, tell these stones to turn into loaves.' But he replied, 'Scripture says: Human beings live not on bread alone but on every word that comes from the mouth of God.' The devil then took him to the holy city and set him on the parapet of the Temple. 'If you are the Son of God,' he said, 'throw yourself down; for scripture says: He has given his angels orders about you, and they will carry you in their arms in case you trip over a stone.' Jesus said to him, 'Scripture also says: Do not put the Lord your God to the test.' Next, taking him to a very high mountain, the devil showed him all the kingdoms of the world and their splendour. And he said to him, 'I will give you all of these, if you fall at my feet and do me homage.' Then Jesus replied, 'Away with you, Satan! For scripture says: The Lord your God is one to whom you must do homage, him alone you must serve.' Then the devil left him, and suddenly angels appeared and looked after him. (Matthew 4:1–11)

Dame Thora reflects

"We only saw the wilderness from the coach but what a stark contrast the Holy Land is between rich and green areas and what the locals call the desert. It's not like the Sahara or pictures from Lawrence of Arabia but it is very barren in parts. The locals have found ways of getting the water into certain areas now though, and I can't walk through Sainsbury's or Marks and Spencer's without seeing all those grapes, tomatoes, avocados and other fruits from Israel. One day they are in the wilderness, the next they are in Marble Arch. Isn't God amazing!

We are tempted, of course we are. There are so many things around that distract us from what he wants us to be and to do – our job is simply to do the best we can and to work hard for God. Jesus teaches us that we should try to avoid temptation. We pray it, don't we, in the Lord's Prayer: 'Lead us not into temptation.'

When I looked from the coach window and saw the region where Jesus had been tempted, I could only look out in amazement and consider just how lucky we are that he was prepared to do all that he did for us. "

Our Hymn

"Everyone knows this hymn, don't they? It is sung at baptisms, weddings and funerals, usually to the tune Crimond. And I was always having requests for this old favourite – a wonderful version of Psalm 23. "

The Lord's my shepherd, I'll not want,
He makes me down to lie.
In pastures green, he leadeth me,
The quiet waters by.

My soul he doth restore again,
And me to walk doth make,
Within the paths of righteousness,
E'en for his own name's sake.

Yea, though I walk in death's dark vale,
Yet will I fear no ill;
For thou art with me and thy rod,
And staff me comfort still.

My table thou has furnished,
In presence of my foes.
My head thou dost with oil anoint,
And my cup overflows.

Goodness and mercy all my life,
Shall surely follow me;
And in God's house, for evermore
My dwelling place shall be.

Prayer
Almighty and everlasting God,
you hate nothing that you have made
and forgive the sins of all those who are penitent.
Create and make in us new and contrite hearts,
that, lamenting our sins
and acknowleding our wretchedness,
we may receive from you, the God of all mercy,
perfect forgiveness and peace:
through Jesus Christ our Lord,
who is alive and reigns with you and the Holy Spirit,
one God, now and forever. Amen.
(Services and Prayers, p. 15, *The Alternative Service Book 1980)*

2

Salvation to This House

JERICHO

In antiquity Jericho was accepted as the oldest city in the world. Set in the midst of the desert – some 36 kilometres north-east of Jerusalem – Jericho is outstanding as a natural oasis amidst so much dry and scorched earth. Even in the winter you can arrive home with a great sun-tan from a stay in Jericho!

Archaeologists have worked in Jericho since 1860, but it was the British-born Kathryn Kenyon who concluded earlier this century that there were about twenty layers indicating successive generations of dwellers in the ancient city. She believed that the earliest ruins dated back to about 8000 BC. The history of Jericho is fascinating. In the Old Testament it is frequently mentioned as a thriving community (for example, Joshua 2–6, 18; 2 Kings 2).

Jericho is an Arab town and between 1967 (when the Israelis occupied the town) and 1994 the community suffered from ongoing and unpredictable conflicts between Jew and Arab. The sense of being 'an oasis' disappeared: shops were boarded up and restaurants closed down. But an agreement between the Israeli Government and the PLO in 1994 has meant that Jericho is currently back under Palestinian control – an event that was happening as Thora visited the Holy Land. Because of security problems on the day we did not actually enter the town but we looked down on the oasis from a distance and Thora was pleased to have seen this famous and historic place.

The well-known site believed to be the Mountain of Temptation can also be viewed better from Jericho. Local people are currently working hard on restoring Jericho as a traditional tourist town where pilgrims will be welcome. The fresh orange juice and bananas here are excellent – but, as everywhere, always take advice from your guide before you eat any fruit!

Reading

They reached Jericho; and as he left Jericho with his disciples and a great crowd, Bartimaeus – that is, the son of Timaeus – a blind beggar, was sitting at the side of the road. When he heard that it was Jesus of Nazareth, he began to shout and cry out, 'Son of David, Jesus, have pity on me.' And many of them scolded him and told him to keep quiet, but he only shouted all the louder, 'Son of David, have pity on me.' Jesus stopped and said, 'Call him here.' So they called the blind man over. 'Courage,' they said, 'get up; he is calling you.' So throwing off his cloak, he jumped up and went to Jesus. Then Jesus spoke, 'What do you want me to do for you?' The blind man said to him; 'Rabbuni, let me see again.' Jesus said to him, 'Go; your faith has saved you.' And at once his sight returned and he followed him along the road. (Mark 10:46–52)

Dame Thora reflects

"We weren't able to go actually into Jericho itself because Yasser Arafat was also due about the same time! The Palestinians had been given the town back after years of Israeli rule. But you could see how lovely the oasis was and this was a town to which Jesus came often. And you could see why. All those lovely trees and plants and shrubs amongst so much dryness. It was quite amazing really.

It was here that Jesus healed the blind man and where Zacchaeus, that little man who was the tax collector climbed up into a sycamore tree to see if he could spot Jesus. We know that Jesus spotted him. I am not too tall myself so I know what he must have felt like. If I was ever in a crowd and couldn't see what was going on I'd always say to Jimmy, 'Tell me what's up then!'

But Jesus' words 'Salvation has come into this house today' are truly wonderful. If only that salvation was in everyone's house. Wouldn't that be something? Our Father spells out his wish that we might all experience something of the light and peace which he brings with him. "

Janette Scott, Dame Thora's daughter and fellow pilgrim.
Janette reflects on the Via Dolorosa in chapter 11

Our Hymn

"This is more of a meditation than a hymn but we had
it on 'Praise Be!' more than once. It's a hymn which
talks about life and pilgrimage every day: say it now as
you read it. **"**

> May the mind of Christ my saviour
> Live in me from day to day,
> By his love and power controlling
> All I do and say.
>
> May the word of God dwell richly
> In my heart from hour to hour,
> So that all may see I triumph
> Only through his power.
>
> May the peace of God my Father
> Rule my life in everything,
> That I may be calm to comfort
> Sick and sorrowing.
>
> May the love of Jesus fill me,
> As the waters fill the sea;
> Him exalting, self abasing,
> This is victory.
>
> May I run the race before me,
> Strong and brave to face the foe,
> Looking only unto Jesus,
> As I onward go.
>
> (Kate B. Wilkinson, 1859–1928)

Prayer

"As we looked out over the city of Jericho and thought about all the conflicts in the world and all the battles and wars that had happened here, I can only remember thinking about how Jesus must have felt as he approached this wonderful oasis. Just sand and rock and stone everywhere and then, suddenly, Jericho, and so I prayed that wonderful prayer of St Francis:"

Lord, make me an instrument of your peace.
Where there is hatred, let me sow love,
Where there is injury, pardon;
Where there is doubt, faith;
Where there is despair, hope;
Where there is darkness, light;
Where there is sadness, joy.
O divine Master, Grant that I may not so much seek
To be consoled, as to console,
To be understood, as to understand,
To be loved, as to love,
For it is in giving that we receive;
It is in pardoning that we are pardoned;
It is in dying that we are born to eternal life.

(St Francis of Assisi, 1181–1226)

3

She Knew It Was the Holy One

BETHLEHEM

A visit to Bethlehem of course is one of the highlights of any pilgrim tour. Dame Thora found her visit an emotional experience as she read the Christmas story just metres away from the place which Christian tradition has long designated as the birthplace of Jesus. I have visited Bethlehem many times and one of the most memorable for me was in the early 1990s when I took my two children,

Stephen and Louisa, to spend Christmas in Bethlehem. It was a simple, often poignant and totally life-changing experience. The tinsel, Christmas tree, cards and turkey meant absolutely nothing. The simplicity of the birth of Jesus remains with me even now.

But the consequences of a visit to Bethlehem are a desire to celebrate and an urge to share with others what one has found. Although the Church of the Nativity, built over the cave housing the birthplace of Jesus, has been reconstructed many times, parts of the present building date back to the sixth century. This, in itself, is something of a miracle. Bethlehem, known in the Old Testament as the City of David, now has a population of Muslim and Christian Arabs, but the Nativity Church is the centre of the community in what in known as 'Manger Square'.

The group was full of expectation when we arrived. Thora had prepared the Bible reading. We had Christmas carols at the ready – in May! It was to be quite a morning.

Reading
Now it happened that at this time Caesar Augustus issued a decree that a census should be made of the whole inhabited world. The census – the first – took place while Quirinius was governor of Syria and everyone went to be registered – each to his own town. So Joseph set out from the town of Nazareth in Galilee for Judea, to David's town called Bethlehem, since he was of David's house and line, in order to be registered together with Mary, his betrothed, who was with child. Now it happened that, while they were there, the time came for her to have her child, and she gave birth to a son, her first-born. She wrapped him in swaddling clothes and laid him in a manger because there was no room for them in the living-space. In the countryside, close by, there

were some shepherds out in the fields keeping guard over their sheep during the watches of the night. An angel of the Lord stood over them and the glory of the Lord shone round them. They were terrified, but the angel said, 'Do not be afraid. Look, I bring you news of great joy, a joy to be shared by the whole people. Today in the town of David a Saviour has been born to you; he is Christ the Lord. And here is a sign for you: you will find a baby wrapped in swaddling clothes and lying in a manger. And all at once with the angel there was a great throng of the hosts of heaven, praising God with the words: Glory to God in the highest heaven, and on earth peace for those he favours. (Luke 2:1–14)

Dame Thora reflects

"This was my second visit to the City of David. I must say that when I went to Bethlehem the first time I could hardly believe it. It's like when you are a child and your mother reads you a lovely fairy story and you think: 'Oh, how marvellous.' I could not believe that I was there. Everything about it led me to believe that of course this was the place where Jesus had been born.

Of course, a lot of people don't believe it. As a matter of fact, when I came back there was a very nice man, quite high up in the church, and I was going out shopping and he met me and put his arm around me and said, 'Did you enjoy your holiday?' And I told him that I had and that I had visited Bethlehem. He asked me outright: Thora, you are a very honest woman – pardon me saying that – do you think that Jesus was born in Bethlehem? And in a flash I said, 'Yes, I do.' And he said, 'I love you, so do I. But there are quite a few people who don't believe that Jesus was born there.' I told him that there was no question about it for me.

That was where Jesus was born. There was only one thing that dimmed it for me. And that was that I wished Jan had been sitting next to me during that time. It would have been lovely. There was a little, young nun next to me praying – she looked about seventeen or eighteen – and she was praying throughout the time we were there. I suppose that I looked at her and wished that Jan had been there praying with us too. Mind you if I see anything beautiful – some flowers or a rose bush – I always wish that other people could share it, be with me there and then.

This time, then, it was lovely to be in Bethlehem with Jan. And when it came to me reading the Christmas story, which I did in the church, I got quite choked up really. Being a woman who has been pregnant and carried a baby I couldn't helping thinking – how must Mary have felt? She must have been saying to herself that she knew she was about to have the baby within the next few hours and there was nowhere for them to go.

And for it to be a stable – one immediately thinks of dirt on the floor. Of course, it wasn't like that. I think of the carol 'Away in a manger, no crib for a bed, the little Lord Jesus lay down his sweet head.' It's one of my favourite carols. And this time Jan was with me. We were holding hands, would you believe it? Throughout our short service we held on to each other. I remember looking at the cross on the altar of the church and thinking about that little baby.

As well as thinking about the infant Jesus, the picture of Mary having the child is very strong when you sit in that church and hear the words from the Bible. The mother looking at her new child and being relieved that it was all over. There is a feeling there that I am not clever enough to describe but Mary felt it in her heart. It's when they pass you your baby wrapped in a bit of cloth and you think, 'It's alive and it's lovely.' It really is a wonderful moment. Mary must have gone through all of that too. I know we think of it all as though it's on a Christmas card but I was thinking of a pregnant woman giving birth to a young child. She knew that it was the Holy One. And there were the animals eating the hay and looking on at this wonderful scene.

As you go down the steps to the star where Christians worship the baby Jesus you feel very excited. I looked at the star and I suppose, being an actress, I have been blessed with just a little more imagination than normal. I looked at the star and I remember thinking about that little child. That is where you were born – you whom we cannot really describe and whom we love so dearly. To stand in front of that star is a great experience. It is a pity that not everyone can stand there and think about what happened on that first Christmas morning.

It brought back so many memories of Christmas. Christmas has always been a great thing with us. As you know, I never had to look for God – he was always there. And this was my mother's example: she wanted us to be Christians and had every intention of us being devout Christians. And yet, my mother who had sung the solos ('I know that my Redeemer liveth') from the Messiah for years (people now, when I go home, still talk about her singing those solos!), taught us that Christmas was a time of great faith and joy. Our door was always open. You came in, you had a drink, whatever we had you could have it. You could smell the apple sauce in the background along with the mincemeat. My mother used to prepare the vegetables for the following day. It was a lovely time of the year. Great.

Everyone has a right to celebrate the way they want. We were so unsophisticated. Our Christmas tree had proper candles: it's a wonder that we didn't set the place on fire! We had a big open fire. And the only time that anything was allowed on the piano was at Christmas – a box of Turkish delight and a little silver dish with sweets in. The basket of fruit was arranged by *moi* with a bit of holly around it. And my father always brought home a box of tangerines on Christmas Eve – a box with some of them wrapped in silver paper, they don't do that now – and a pineapple – a pineapple, in Morecambe! And ten records from House's Music Shop – every Christmas Eve. You didn't have to say, 'Dad, you won't forget the records or the pineapple?' That was his donation and we loved him.

Being in the entertainment business, as my father was, he had a lot of business with one of the whisky distillers and every Christmas they used to send him a turkey. Another firm would send him a goose. And we always chose to have the goose on Christmas Day and the goose grease was put into a jamjar for during the winter. Being on the coast, it was handy to have to rub on your chest if you needed it. All you had to do was come home from school with a bit of a cough and – 'Oh, you are going to be rubbed with goose grease.'

The big thing of Christmas in our house was a trip to the cemetery. My sister was knocked down and killed by a motor bike and sidecar and she was buried on the very day that she would have been six. She was buried in the old cemetery in the grave next to my grandfather and grandmother. Between 10.30 and 11.00 on Christmas morning my father, my brother and I set off with the wreath and we walked to the old church and the cemetery and we had to pass the street where my Auntie

Lizzie lived. And my Auntie Lizzie was a midwife and she had brought hundreds of babies into the world. But at Christmas, next to the fireplace there was always some beef tea on the go: that was for the mother after the birth. We would always have a glass of ginger wine and a piece of homemade cake and by the time we got home my mother would be preparing the dinner. Then we used to look at all our presents again. It was magic.

All of this came back to me in Bethlehem. I am thinking of Jesus being born. It is called Christmas Day because of Jesus. We sang 'Once in royal David's city' and 'O come, all ye faithful'. It's funny, isn't it, how people like carols because they don't actually think that they are hymns. We know different but they don't. You get the people who are against religion and often they don't mind singing a carol. But carols are Christmas hymns.

At home we used to sing them in harmony because they were professional people. As kids we would go around Christmas carolling and, I suppose, we were begging really. We'd go to Dr Waterson's who always had a £5 bag of new gilt pennies. And, of course, you always left to the end: 'Christmas is coming, the goose is getting fat; please put a penny in the old man's hat.' Then you always sang the next bit with real pathos: 'If you haven't got a penny, then a halfpenny will do.' But we always put plenty into the last line: 'If you haven't got a halfpenny, then God bless you.' This was just in case they weren't going to give you anything.

When we sang 'Once in royal' in Bethlehem I always think about the many times that I have heard that carol with the first verse as a solo. When my grand-daughter was at school we went to the carol concert in Chichester and, like any other grandmother, I am going to say that Daisy had a beautiful voice – but it's the truth, she does. And she was chosen to do the solo. And when her voice started to sing from the back I put my arm through Jan's and I was trembling, trying not to cry, but I did and it didn't matter. And when we sang it in Bethlehem I remembered my family and I was very happy.

A few weeks ago we were in Chichester Cathedral and the geography of it means that you can sit behind the choir. I looked across and I remembered the night that Daisy had sung there and the visit to Bethlehem all rolled into one. I forget what hymn it was. But I was crying, and everyone saw me. Mind you, I cry at anything. Choirboys can upset me too – I mean they can move me; you know what I mean.

So back to the lovely town of Bethlehem – a must for all Christian people if ever they can get there. It all started here and it is lovely. I can remember the market square and the little door into the Church of the Nativity. I looked around that lovely Palestinian town and asked myself, 'Was it really like this in Jesus' day?' It is an amazing thought. Of course it would not have been quite the same, but the equivalent of today. All the time I was there I was thinking how different our Christmas would be from now on. **"**

Our Hymns

Once in royal David's city
Stood a lowly cattle shed,
Where a mother laid her baby
In a manger for his bed;
Mary was that mother mild,
Jesus Christ her little child.

She Knew It Was the Holy One

He came down from earth to heaven,
Who is God and Lord of all,
And his shelter was a stable,
And his cradle was a stall;
With the poor and mean and lowly
Lived on earth our Saviour holy.

And through all his wondrous childhood
He would honour and obey,
Love and watch the lowly maiden,
In whose gentle arms he lay;
Christian children all must be
Mild, obedient, good as he.

For he is our childhood's pattern,
Day by day like us he grew,
He was little, weak and helpless,
Tears and smiles like us he knew;
And he feeleth for our sadness,
And he shareth in our gladness.

And our eyes at last shall see him,
Through his own redeeming love,
For that child so dear and gentle
Is our Lord in heaven above;
And he leads his children on
To the place where he is gone.

(Mrs C. F. Alexander, 1823–95)

O come, all ye faithful, Joyful and triumphant,
O come ye, O come ye to Bethlehem.
Come and behold him, born the King of Angels.
O come, let us adore him, Christ the Lord!

God of God, Light of Light,
Lo, he abhors not the virgin's womb.
Very God, begotten not created.
O come, let us adore him, Christ the Lord!

Sing, choirs of angels, Sing in exultation,
Sing, all ye citizens of heaven above.
Glory to God, in the highest.
O come, let us adore him, Christ the Lord!

Yea, Lord, we greet thee, born this happy morning;
Jesu, to thee be glory given.
Word of the Father, now in flesh appearing.
O come, let us adore him, Christ the Lord!

(Tr. F. Oakeley and others)

Prayer
❝We heard this lovely prayer from the old Book of Common Prayer and I always think it is great at Christmas. ❞

Almighty God, who hast given us thy only-begotten Son to take our nature upon him, and as at this time to be born of a pure virgin; Grant that we being regenerate, and made thy children by adoption and grace, may daily be renewed by thy Holy Spirit; through the same our Lord Jesus Christ, who liveth and reigneth with thee and the same Spirit, ever one God, world without end. Amen.

4

Lazarus Raised

BETHANY

Bethany is a delightful little town which is probably no bigger now than it was in the time of Jesus, though the number of people living in the area around Bethany is increasing all the time. Situated on the eastern slopes of the Mount of Olives, this Arab community has seen a good deal of unrest and uncertainty during the twentieth century.

In the New Testament, there are several key references to the town. It was where Mary and Martha lived and it was where Lazarus was placed in a tomb before Jesus raised him from the dead. In the fourth century a church was built over the traditional site of Lazarus' tomb and this place is preserved today by local inhabitants. There is also a gift shop and a small reconstructed house such as the one which Mary and Martha may have lived in, along with their families and animals.

The churches in Bethany are worth a visit. The Greek Orthodox church is small but delightful. The Roman Catholic church dates from 1954 but there are ruins of buildings from the fifth and twelfth centuries in the courtyard. Inside the church you will find bright mosaics depicting the stories of Luke 10 and John 11.

Reading

Jesus was at Bethany in the house of Simon, a man who had suffered from a virulent skin-disease, when a woman came to him with an alabaster jar of very expensive ointment, and poured it on his head as he was at table. When they saw this, the disciples said indignantly, 'Why this waste? This could have been sold for a high price and the money given to the poor.' But Jesus noticed this and said, 'Why are you upsetting this woman? What she has done for me is indeed a good work! You have the poor with you always, but you will not always have me. When she poured this ointment on my body, she did it to prepare me for burial. In truth I tell you, wherever in all the world this gospel is proclaimed, what she has done will be told as well, in remembrance of her.'
(Matthew 26:6–13)

Dame Thora reflects

"The story of Lazarus is one of those magical ones from the Bible that I can remember as a child. This man had died but Jesus would not be put off. He wanted to come and pay tribute to him himself and to show others something of this new life which he had been talking about. When Lazarus is raised from the dead the word about Jesus' power must have gone all round, not only Jerusalem which we were getting closer and closer to, but back to those towns and villages in Galilee which our double-decker had already visited. In those days, without television, radio and the newspapers, news still travelled pretty fast. Not as fast as today of course, but people got to know and the word went round.

When you visit Bethany, the home town of Mary and Martha, it is the tomb of Lazarus which stands out. I couldn't manage all the steps down to the bottom of the tomb but those who did go down said it was a wonderful experience and there is an obvious link between what Jesus did here and what happened on Calvary. I'll leave that to you to think about! "

Our Hymn

"Frances Havergal was born in 1836 and she lived until 1879. She had a very strong Christian faith and always insisted that she lived out her hymns in her life. So, reading the words of the hymn that we sang at Bethany, you can see how devout she was. Remember Lazarus – he thanked Jesus for his new life. We can do the same as we sing or say the words of this hymn. "

Take my life, and let it be
Consecrated, Lord, to thee;

Take my moments and my days
Let them flow in ceaseless praise.

Take my hands and let them move
At the impulse of thy love.
Take my feet, and let them be
Swift and beautiful for thee.

Take my voice and let me sing
Always, only, for my King;
Take my lips, and let them be
Filled with messages from thee.

Take my silver and my gold;
Not a mite would I withhold;
Take my intellect, and use
Every power as thou shalt choose.

Take my will, and make it thine:
It shall be no longer mine.
Take my heart; it is thine own:
It shall be thy royal throne.

Take my love; my Lord, I pour
At thy feet its treasure store.
Take myself, and I will be
Ever, only, all for thee.

(Frances Ridley Havergal, 1836–79)

Prayer
"Our prayer at Bethany was one of those that we all had to respond to and, bearing in mind what actually

happened at Bethany, it was lovely. Jesus is reminded of
his own death and prays for others.   **„**

O Merciful God, who answerest the poor,
Answer us.
O Merciful God, who answerest the lowly in Spirit,
Answer us.
O Merciful God, who answerest the broken of heart,
Answer us.
O Merciful God,
Answer us.
O Merciful God,
Have compassion.
O Merciful God,
Redeem.
O Merciful God,
Save.
O Merciful God, have pity on us,
Now, speedily,
And at a near time.

(For the Day of Atonement. *The Oxford & Cambridge Office
Book*, p. 210)

5

Now I Am Standing Where He Walked

JERUSALEM

Jerusalem is surely the most fascinating city on earth. Every visit to the Holy City is special. It is a city of faith and hope – a great place of pilgrimage. If God lives in any city he must live in Jerusalem. It is the capital city of the modern state of Israel. During the biblical period it was the capital of both the kingdoms of Judea and Israel. In the time of Abraham it was called Shalem; in later centuries it became known as Yerushalem. Jews flock to the Holy City and approach the Western Wall of the Temple with a variety of emotions, ranging from sadness to sheer joy. Just above the Western Wall, Muslims approach the mosques of the Temple area with a similar sense of having arrived in the Holy City. A few hundred yards away, Christians continually gather in the Church of the Holy Sepulchre to remember the crucifixion and resurrection of Jesus.

Pilgrims have always been drawn to Jerusalem. And we all know that pilgrimage can be tough and demanding. A visit to this historic city can be an exhausting experience, spiritually and emotionally. Jerusalem is situated in the heights of the Judean mountains. It is about 800 metres above sea level and enjoys slightly milder temperatures than Tel Aviv and Galilee.

In the first century AD Josephus reports that a census taken during the Feast of Tabernacles revealed more than 2.7 million people in the city as pilgrims. When Constantine converted to Christianity in AD 313 and the Christian faith was officially adopted by the Roman Empire, there was a rapid increase in the number of Christian symbols and treasures to be found there. St Helena arrived in 327 and immediately set about identifying the places associated with Jesus and since then many Christian pilgrims have been happy to follow the tradition she set.

The Church Fathers make frequent reference to the Holy City. Gregory of Nyssa condemned the extreme licentiousness of the pilgrims he had seen in Jerusalem. St Augustine warned pilgrims to wander with their heart and not their feet. It is, of course, possible to write a whole book on Jerusalem itself. We must concentrate here on the particular places which are visited by thousands of pilgrims from all over the world every day of every year. Before the 1967 war, the border between Israel and Jordan ran right through the centre of modern Jerusalem. Israel recaptured the old city in 1967 and, despite the momentous moves towards peace in the 1990s between Jordan and Israel after more than two decades of hostility, Jerusalem remains a divided city as far as its population is concerned. East and West Jerusalem have very different populations. The streets are full of different-looking people with a remarkable variety of styles of dress. Very few local buses run from one side to the other, though there have been many improvements in communications.

The Israeli Government has embarked on a massive building policy on the outskirts of Jerusalem. Several satellite towns have been built within a few minutes of the centre of Jerusalem. The population has increased as Jews have arrived from all over the world. Apparently, from the air, Jerusalem will soon look like David's star.

Within the walls of the old city you will find a rich diversity of people, impressive architecture (both ancient and modern) and colourful markets. There is also an intriguing range of aromas as spicy food is cooked and consumed in cafes and at street vendors' stalls. A map of the old city shows its famous four quarters. The modern centre of Jerusalem has a pedestrianised area around Ben Yehuda Street where pilgrims can enjoy a late night coffee and ice cream and calmly watch the world go by. There are many good hotels, an excellent bus network, many museums, galleries and historic places which make a pilgrimage to Jerusalem a unique and memorable experience. Some people comment on how modern the place has become and how it can sometimes seem to be over-commercialised. But never let this get in the way of your pilgrimage. 'One has to realize, I suppose, that to some people Jesus Christ is merely a name, to some an historical character only, yet surely visitors to Jerusalem must be sufficiently educated to know that it is a Holy City.' (Angela du Maurier, *Pilgrims by the Way*)

An unusual view of Jerusalem

Reading

I rejoiced that they said to me, 'Let us go to the house of Yahweh.' At last our feet are standing at your gates, Jerusalem! Jerusalem, built as a city, is one united whole, there the tribes go up, the tribes of the Lord, a sign for Israel to give thanks to the name of the Lord.

For there are set thrones of judgement, the thrones of the house of David. Pray for the peace of Jerusalem, prosperity for your homes! Peace within your walls, prosperity in your palaces! For love of my brothers and my friends I will say 'Peace upon you!' For love of the house of the Lord your God I will pray for your well-being. (Psalm 122)

Dame Thora reflects

❝When we arrived in the Holy City we saw the Golden Dome and the churches. The only way I can personally describe how it feels to be in Jerusalem is to say: 'I am standing here. He came to Jerusalem. Of that there is no doubt. And now I am standing here where he walked.' So if you have not been to Jerusalem you can't have that thought but you can remember that everyone you love might one day be there. And this is the Holy City for Jews, Muslims and Christians.

Of course, I will never forget the treatment of the Jews during the Second World War and I think that people sometimes forget that too easily. I couldn't imagine anyone treating anyone like that. I found myself looking at some of the lovely faces in Jerusalem whilst I was there and wondering what some of the families had been through. The Yad Vashem Museum is a fitting memorial to such an appalling thing. The Jews had come from all over the world: and you would see the tiny boys and the little girls – all children are lovely in their own way. The Jewish people are a family people. They are a close-knit community. They teach us a lot. I often found it hard to work out who was a Jew and who was an Arab. Don't get me wrong, some of the skins are the same colour and Hebrew and Arabic both have similar sounds. But they are very handsome races and it was lovely to see the youngsters, both the Jews and the Arabs.

There was nothing about it which to me was not steeped in history. And as I looked out over the Holy City I couldn't help wondering what Jesus saw: something very similar, no doubt. 'O Pray for the peace of Jerusalem' it says in the Psalms and that is what we did. And every time we used that lovely word, 'shalom' – peace be with you.

My imagination is always important to me. When I used to go to Sunday School as a child no one enjoyed it more than me, no one. I loved it every week. I enjoyed sitting there listening to the stories from the Bible and it was great – I loved it. So to hear the stories in Jerusalem itself is quite amazing. I have never been able to understand, when there is one God with the Son he gave us to show us how much he loves us, why there is so much division. I find it difficult.

In these days people travel all over the world. Mrs Smith and her husband can pick where they want to go. Benidorm, if you like. There are some lovely places to be. You can go and have a good time. But there is something so special about the Holy Land. **”**

Our Hymn
“Whenever the royal family go to church I think this is the hymn I hear the most often. In our own national

life in Britain it is a hymn which talks about God unchanging whilst other things change. Isaac Watts – born in 1674 – wrote hundreds of hymns but his most famous is the one I remembered as we arrived in the Holy City. **"**

> O God, our help in ages past,
> Our hope for years to come,
> Our shelter from the stormy blast,
> And our eternal home.
>
> Under the shadow of thy throne
> Thy saints have dwelt secure;
> Sufficient is thine arm alone,
> And our defence is sure.
>
> Before the hills in order stood,
> Or earth received her frame,
> From everlasting thou art God,
> To endless years the same.
>
> A thousand ages in thy sight
> Are like an evening gone;
> Short as the watch that ends the night
> Before the rising sun.
>
> Time, like an ever-rolling stream,
> Bears all its sons away;
> They fly forgotten, as a dream
> Dies at the opening day.
>
> (Isaac Watts, 1674–1748)

Prayer
Eternal God, Father of all mankind,
You have shown yourself to the world in many ways,
and have never left yourself without witness in the lives of
    men:
Hear our prayer for people
whose faith and customs differ from ours.
Make us ready to learn from them,
and also eager to share wth them
the riches of your truth, which you have given us
in Jesus Christ our Lord. Amen.

(*New Every Morning*, p. 117)

6

Full of the Thoughts of People

THE TEMPLE AREA

The Wailing (or Western) Wall is one of the most famous of Jerusalem's religious sites and is easily accessible through the streets of the Jewish Quarter or you can take a bus or a taxi and approach the Wall through specially constructed gates. You are asked to remember that this is the holiest of all places for the Jewish community. No pictures, for instance, should be taken during the sabbath period. Since 1967, the space immediately in front of the Wall has been cleared to create a massive square where many major public events can now take place within the old city.

The Wall (which is 48 metres long and 18 metres high) is the only surviving part of the magnificent Temple built by Herod. It is situated just below the Temple area where the Golden Dome (now a mosque) sits impressively. The Al Aqsa Mosque is also on the Temple area site. The title 'Wailing Wall' comes from the lamentations of the Jews, passed from one generation to another, when they pray that the Temple may be once again restored. As you look at the Wall you see the men praying on the left, the women on the right. This is a scene of Jerusalem. The tradition of praying at the Wall goes back to the destruction of the Temple in around AD 70.

Even today the wall is often a focal point of ongoing tension between Arab and Jew because of the close proximity of the two important holy sites. The Golden Dome sits above a site which was extensively developed by Herod the Great (37–4 BC). In the time of Jesus the Temple must have been a magnificent building. The Golden Dome, recently renovated by an expert team from Belfast, dominates the Jerusalem landscape and is a worldwide symbol of the Holy City.

It was in the seventh century that the site fell into Muslim hands and the first mosques were built. Tradition suggests that the Prophet Muhammad was taken up to heaven from the rock which the dome covers; this was where he received the Qur'an from Allah. Shoes have to be removed and all hand luggage left with a member of your group before you can proceed into the mosques above the Western Wall.

Dame Thora reflects

"I had never seen the Wailing Wall before. I had thought for a long time about this holy place for the Jews. I

Dame Thora and her late husband, Jimmy, in Jerusalem

would like to know a lot more about it but I stood and looked from a good way off, the men praying on one side and the women on the other. I can remember watching them praying and thinking, 'This is wonderful. It's marvellous to be here.' A couple of months before we left I was talking to someone who had been and prayed in front of the Western Wall and they told me how much it had moved them. And I could understand that. The Wailing Wall is full of the thoughts of people. There was so much religious activity, so much to see at the Wailing Wall. So much had happened there.

The addition, of course, of the six flames next to the six stars of David is very moving – each one representing a million Jews killed during the Holocaust. These lights never go out: the fire does not stop burning. It is amazing to look at the Wall and then at the stars and think that this has been here for so long. It is incredible. Here we are in 1994: the black hats and the hair in locks – the Orthodox tradition. Jesus himself was a Jew and they are a very special and often misunderstood people.

The Golden Dome is, of course, Jerusalem itself to many people. It is what you see on posters and postcards. I didn't actually climb up there to visit the mosques; I sat on a wall and watched the Jews praying and wondered if God had a sense of humour. He must have – with all these different faiths and beliefs. He loves us just the same. **"**

Our Hymn
" Most of the requests for this hymn on 'Praise Be!' used to come from couples who had it at their weddings and who were celebrating a wedding anniversary. It's a wedding hymn, of course, but it is also a hymn of praise

to God our Father. It was written by Henry Francis Lyte who was a curate and it is based on the words of Psalm 103. And with all the faith and hope that one finds in God in Jerusalem this was the hymn we sang in front of the Western Wall. **"**

Praise, my soul, the King of heaven;
To his feet thy tribute bring.
Ransomed, healed, restored, forgiven,
Who like me his praise should sing?
Praise him! Praise him! Praise him! Praise him!
Praise the everlasting King.

Praise him for his grace and favour
To our fathers in distress;
Praise him, still the same for ever,
Slow to chide and swift to bless:
Praise him! Praise him! Praise him! Praise him!
Glorious in his faithfulness.

Father-like, he tends and spares us;
Well our feeble frame he knows;
In his hands he gently bears us,
Rescues us from all our foes.
Praise him! Praise him! Praise him! Praise him!
Widely as his mercy flows.

Angels, help us to adore him!
Ye behold him face to face;
Sun and moon, bow down before him;
Dwellers all in time and space.
Praise him! Praise him! Praise him! Praise him!
Praise with us the God of grace.

(H. F. Lyte, 1793–1847)

7

Poor Peter Denied Jesus

ST PETER IN GALLICANTU

Mount Zion can be very disappointing if you imagined a high, dominating mountain on the outskirts of Jerusalem. It is in fact a small mound within the built-up area of the city and it is hard to differentiate it from the buildings around. It was designated Mount Zion in the Byzantine period but it is not the Mount Zion associated with King David's time.

The Church of St Anne and the Room of the Last Supper are both on the mount, but the highlight of any visit here must be to cross the road and enter the Church of St Peter in Gallicantu, the Church of the Cock Crowing. Although some find the interior of the church loud and even gaudy, I always find it a refreshing place during the tour of Mount Zion. The mosaics on the walls and ceiling are modern but imaginative. But it is the area beneath the church which attracts most attention because tradition has pinpointed the small rooms and cells beneath the church as those of Caiaphas' house (the High Priest in the time of Jesus) where Our Lord was taken after his arrest. From here Jesus would have been brought to the soldiers at 'the pavement'.

Once the group had arrived in the lowest part of the small rooms we read the following passage from the Bible and sang a hymn. Jesus, a prisoner? This can be a very emotional part of the pilgrimage to Jerusalem.

Reading
While Peter was down below in the courtyard, one of the high priest's servant-girls came up. She saw Peter warming himself there, looked closely at him and said, 'You too were with Jesus, the man from Nazareth.' But he denied it. 'I do not know. I do not understand what you are talking about,' he said. And he went out into the forecourt, and a cock crowed. The servant-girl saw him and again started telling the bystanders, 'This man is one of them.' But again he denied it. A little later the bystanders themselves said to Peter, 'You are certainly one of them! Why, you are a Galilean.' But he started cursing and swearing. 'I do not know the man you speak of.' And at once the cock crowed for the second time, and Peter recalled what Jesus had said to him, 'Before the cock crows twice, you will have disowned me three times.' And he burst into tears. (Mark 14:66–72)

Dame Thora reflects
"I must admit that sometimes I found the geography of Jerusalem confusing. I mean, in the Bible, everything sounds as if it is quite a way off but when you are actually there you realise that most of the main things happened within walking distance. For instance, the Garden of Gethsemane is near to this place – the Church of the Cock Crowing (What a name!) – and Jesus was taken to the start of the Via Dolorosa which is not that far away from here either.

Now I sat in the church whilst the group went down more than a hundred steps into the prison house beneath the church. The modern colourful mosaics were moving enough for me but Jan told me how meaningful it was actually to go down to the level of Jesus and see the kind of place – cold, dark and miserable – where Jesus was put after he had been arrested.

Being in prison must be a terrible thing. I have had many letters from people who have had relatives in prison, and maybe, however rotten and silly the things they have done, we can't begin to understand what loss of freedom really means. For Jesus it must have been even worse because he could have left the place. We know he had the power to walk out at any time but he recognised the extent of man's folly and had to go along with all the pain and anguish which followed.

And poor Peter. Remember, it is here, in this place, in the courtyard above, that Peter did what we all do at times, often without realising it. He denied his Lord. He said that he had never met him, did not know what they were talking about. It is a sad business but you can understand human weakness when you look at Peter here. He was afraid, scared, worried about what was going to happen to him and the other disciples. The wonderful teaching and promises which he had heard in Galilee a few days ago – where were they now? What an appropriate place this is to understand us and God together. God give us strength. **"**

Our Hymn

"It is a good thing that our young people feel that we can sing hymns which have a real rhythm and tune to them. And this one, sung in the prison cell where Jesus may have been kept on his last night, is a very challenging one. God has forgiven us in his Son. We sang this with gusto. **"**

131

God forgave my sin in Jesus' name.
I've been born again in Jesus' name.
And in Jesus' name I come to you
To share his love as he told me to.
    He said, 'Freely, freely, you have received.
    Freely, freely give.
    Go in my name and because you believe
    Others will know that I live.

All pow'r is giv'n in Jesus' name.
In earth and heav'n in Jesus' name.
And in Jesus' name I come to you
To share his pow'r as he told me to.

(Carol Owens)

8

The Family Prayer

PATER NOSTER

Situated on the Mount of Olives, the Pater Noster Church is one of those gems you are unlikely to forget on your return home. The Mount of Olives is to the east of Jerusalem and rises some 100 metres above the Holy City. The church is situated within an elegant courtyard with a garden (which has seen better days) and it makes a refreshing change from the graffiti seen so much outside this tranquil area. The original church on this site was destroyed by the Persians in about 614 and the Crusaders then built a small chapel which has always represented the place where Jesus taught his disciples about prayer and how to pray (Luke 11:2–4). A French princess arrived here in the late nineteenth century and reported that the site had once again become derelict.

Today the whole of the courtyard and the church contains wall tiles on which the Lord's Prayer is written in more than eighty languages. Each pilgrim group looks for their own – Italian, Spanish, Russian, French, English, Greek, and so on. All around the courtyard the Lord's Prayer is being said in different languages.

Reading

'In your prayers do not babble as the gentiles do, for they think that by using many words they will make themselves heard. Do not be like them; your Father knows what you need before you ask him. So you should pray like this: Our Father in heaven, may your name be holy, your kingdom come, your will be done, on earth as in heaven. Give us today our daily bread. And forgive us our debts, as we have forgiven those who are in debt to us. And do not put us to the test, but save us from the Evil One.' (Matthew 6:7–13)

Dame Thora reflects

"From a very early age indeed I learnt how to pray. My mother used to tell us that it was right and even to this day I actually talk – and I mean talk – to God. I often say to him, 'Oh, I know you know all this already' or 'I have told you this so many times before, but . . .' and

he never tires of listening. God listens to us and we have
to learn to listen to him.

Shortly after the pilgrimage, when Jimmy was poorly
in hospital I used to come home in the evening and say
my prayers. I would literally talk to God about the
situation and, do you know, he answered my prayers.
He gave me answers as he has always done. Not always
in the way that we would like but in other ways: God
is good.

The Lord's Prayer is a wonderful prayer because it
sums up the whole of life: it teaches us to ask forgiveness
and to forgive, and not to take anything for granted. It
really is wonderful. **"**

Our Hymn

"Whenever I think of this hymn I think of the phrase
'Be our strength in hours of weakness'. Whatever prayer
we offer to God, whether we are up or down, he hears
our prayer and strengthens us. **"**

> Father, hear the prayer we offer:
> Not for ease that prayer shall be,
> But for strength that we may ever
> Live our lives courageously.
>
> Not for ever in green pastures
> Do we ask our way to be:
> But by steep and rugged pathways
> Would we strive to climb to thee.
>
> Not for ever by still waters
> Would we idly quiet stay;

135

But would smite the living fountains
From the rocks along the way.

Be our strength in hours of weakness,
In our wanderings be our guide;
Through endeavour, failure, danger,
Father, be thou at our side.

Let our path be bright or dreary,
Storm or sunshine be our share;
May our souls in hope unweary,
Make thy work our ceaseless prayer.
(Love Maria Willis, 1824–1908)

Prayer
Our Father, who art in heaven, hallowed be thy name, thy
Kingdom come, thy will be done on earth as it is in heaven.
Give us this day our daily bread, and forgive us our tres-
passes, as we forgive them that trespass against us. And lead
us not into temptation, but deliver us from evil. For thine is
the kingdom, the power and the glory, for ever and ever,
Amen.

9

Bone Boxes and Tears

DOMINUS FLEVIT

The site of this church is one of the most beautiful in the
Holy Land. Perched on the Mount of Olives, overlooking the Temple area, Dominus Flevit represents the place
where Jesus looked out over the city of Jerusalem and wept.
There is a remarkable view of the Holy City from this point

and the church is designed so as to add to the drama of a pilgrimage here.

The name Dominus Flevit means 'The Lord wept'. The current church (known locally as the Tear Drop Church) was built in 1955. The architect of this church – and of many others in the Holy Land today – was Barluzzi. The foundations date back to the fifth century and a mosaic from the earlier building can be seen on the left of the entrance. During excavations before the present church was built, a number of small boxes containing bones of the dead were found. On the side of some of these 'bone boxes' there were small crosses, confirming the presence of Christians in the Holy City in those early centuries. You can see these boxes just inside the gate at the entrance to the magnificent garden.

When Barluzzi designed the church he departed from the usual practice of placing the altar at the east. Instead the altar faces west, looking out dramatically over the Kidron Valley towards the Dome of the Rock.

Reading

As he drew near and came in sight of the city he shed tears over it and said, 'If you too had only recognised on this day the way to peace! But in fact it is hidden from your eyes! Yes, a time is coming when your enemies will raise fortifications all round you, when they will encircle you and hem you in on every side; they will dash you and the children inside your walls to the ground; they will leave not one stone standing on another within you, because you did not recognise the moment of your visitation.' (Luke 19:41–44)

A view of the Mount of Olives

Dame Thora reflects

"Now this is a special place – on the Mount of Olives overlooking the Temple Area. It is a steep climb down the mount and all I can remember was the lovely face of an elderly Arab gentleman standing inside the garden. He was guarding the bone boxes. What a thought!

The remains of people were put into small boxes and then they were buried with a symbol and a name on them. There were many names on those boxes from the New Testament times and some of them had a cross on them too – so there you are!

You go along a winding pathway, with breathtaking views of Jerusalem. In the garden of Dominus Flevit you really know that you are in the Holy City. Wonderful views. Absolutely magnificent. Then we turned a sharpish right into the church itself which has its altar facing the wrong way. The church is in the shape of a tear drop because it was here that Jesus wept over the city of Jerusalem.

When you sit down inside the church there is no noise. No cars or lorries, people – nothing. The silence is wonderful. And the window behind the altar focuses on the view that Jesus would have seen when he arrived in Jerusalem and cried over the city. I felt a bit like he did in Nazareth, but I can fully understand why Jesus wanted to weep. After all, God is so good, so wonderful, and the world is such a hard place to be in sometimes. He knew what was ahead and he faced it with real courage. And whatever the future holds for us, we should do the same. "

Our Hymn

"As a Wesleyan, in Morecambe, for me this hymn has

very special memories and as we sang it, looking out from Dominus Flevit, I realised what a friend Jesus really is. What an immense strength in an often difficult world. And, don't forget – carry everything to God in prayer! **99**

What a friend we have in Jesus,
All our sin and grief to bear!
What a privilege to carry
Everything to God in prayer!
O what peace we often forfeit,
O what needless pain we bear –
All because we do not carry
Everything to God in prayer!

Have we trials and temptations?
Is there trouble everywhere?
We should never be discouraged:
Take it to the Lord in prayer!
Can we find a friend so faithful,
Who will all our sorrows share?
Jesus knows our every weakness –
Take it to the Lord in prayer!

Are we weak and heavy-laden,
Cumbered with a load of care?
Jesus only is our refuge,
Take it to the Lord in prayer!
Do thy friends despise, forsake thee?
Take it to the Lord in prayer!
In His arms He'll take and shield thee,
Thou wilt find a solace there.

(Joseph Scriven, 1819–1886)

Prayer

O God, the God of all goodness and grace, who art worthy of a greater love than we can either give or understand; fill our hearts, we beseech thee, with such love towards thee as may cast out sloth and fear, that nothing may seem too hard for us to do or suffer in obedience to thee; and grant that by thus loving, we may become daily more like unto thee, and finally obtain the crown of life, which thou hast promised to those who unfeignedly love thee; through Jesus Christ our Lord. Amen.

(George Appleton, *Daily Prayer and Praise*, p. 78)

10

Agony on the Rock

THE GARDEN OF GETHSEMANE

The Garden of Gethsemane evokes strong passions in any reader of the final days of Jesus' human life in the gospels. It is here that Jesus comes to pray, here that he meditates on his future destiny, and in this very garden that he is betrayed.

Today, the garden is part of the Mount of Olives. The Church of All Nations is situated to the right of the garden as you look down on it from the Temple area. It is called 'All Nations' because donations were received from Roman Catholics all over the world to build this church. In the sanctuary of the church is a large rock jutting out of the ground. Tradition suggests that this was the rock on which Jesus rested the night before he was taken away.

There has been a church here since the fourth century, but the present one dates back to 1924 and you will always remember it for its sombre light. In fact, after the bright, Middle Eastern sunshine it often takes several minutes before you can focus inside the dark church and finding other members of your group can be a problem. Do remember that the Franciscans expect silence in this church though they do allow flash bulbs to be used for photographs.

Reading

They came to a plot of land called Gethsemane, and he said to his disciples, 'Stay here while I pray.' Then he took Peter and James and John with him. And he began to feel terror and anguish. And he said to them, 'My soul is sorrowful to the point of death. Wait here and stay awake.' And going on a little further he threw himself to the ground and prayed that, if it were possible, this hour might pass him by. 'Abba, Father!' he said. 'For you everything is possible. Take this cup away from me. But let it be as you, not I, would have it.' He came back and found them sleeping and said to Peter, 'Simon, are you asleep? Had you not the strength to stay awake one hour? Stay awake and pray not to be put to the test. The spirit is willing enough, but human nature is weak.' Again he went away and prayed, saying the same words. And once more he came back and found them sleeping, their eyes were so heavy; and they could find no answer for him. He came back a third time and said to them, 'You can sleep on now and have your rest. It is all over. The hour has come. Now the Son of Man is to be betrayed into the hands of sinners. Get up! Let us go! My betrayer is not far away.'
(Mark 14:32–42)

Dame Thora reflects

"This was one of the few places that I had visited before, when I came to film in the Holy Land for the BBC. There is not much light inside the church and when you first go in it is difficult to see exactly where you are going.

It's not much of a garden outside now – just a few lovely plants and trees which Jimmy and I looked at. But the whole area reminds you of Jesus' final few days before his crucifixion. He had come down from

144

Capernaum, where we had spent the lovely days around the Sea of Galilee; he had wept, up there, over the city and now he was down here about to be arrested. It is a terrible thing that the Son of God was betrayed in this way but God knew what he was going to do about it. What began in Gethsemane would change the course of history. What a moment it would be!

I also remember that Reverend Rob had told us that Peter, James and John were special amongst the twelve and that at special times he chose the three of them to understand things better so that they could explain it to the others. I mean, twelve is a lot of people to have around you all the time.

So it was that Peter, James and John were with Jesus again, and Peter is as excitable as ever – God bless him. But if you have ever been betrayed – if the trust you had in someone suddenly breaks down – perhaps you can begin to experience the agony which Jesus must have endured on the rock inside the church. I will never forget Gethsemane. **"**

Our Hymn

"Every Holy Week this is one of the best hymns in the hymn book. It talks about the passion of Jesus but in a way that reminds us of all the characters and drama that surrounded it. We sang it in Gethsemane as an act of faith. **"**

My song is love unknown,
My Saviour's love to me;
Love to the loveless shown,
That they might lovely be.

The Garden of Gethsemane

Agony on the Rock

O, who am I,
That for my sake,
My Lord should take
Frail flesh and die?

He came from his blest throne,
Salvation to bestow;
But men made strange, and none
The longed-for Christ would know.
But O, my friend!
My friend indeed,
Who at my need
His life did spend.

Sometimes they strew his way,
And his sweet praises sing;
Resounding all the day,
Hosannas to their King.
Then 'Crucify!'
Is all their breath,
And for his death
They thirst and cry.

Why, what has my Lord done?
What makes this rage and spite?
He made the lame to run,
He gave the blind their sight.
Sweet injuries!
Yet they at these
Themselves displease,
And 'gainst him rise.

They rise and needs will have
My dear Lord made away;

A murderer they save;
The Prince of Life they slay.
Yet cheerful he
To suffering goes,
That he his foes
From thence might free.

Here might I stay and sing,
No story so divine;
Never was love, dear King,
Never was grief like thine.
This is my friend,
In whose sweet praise
I all my days
Could gladly spend.

(Samuel Crossman, 1624–83)

Prayer
Was that my Gethsemane hour?
Was that my Gethsemane hour,
As I agonized in confusion of thought?
Or my abandonment upon the cross
When thought itself seemed dead?
Was it not rather I who knew Him not?
Or hastened up a hill to hurl this wretched body
From a gallows tree of my own making,
Or my disbelief?
There is no certainty but this –
He caught me as I fell.

(Petya Christie)

11

The Path of Suffering

THE VIA DOLOROSA

I have no doubt in recommending the Via Dolorosa (the Way of Sorrows) as a spiritual discipline which should be undertaken by every Christian where possible during their lifetime. It is the most life-changing and challenging experience for any believer. It is officially carried out by the Franciscans at 3.00 pm every Friday but pilgrim groups can be seen doing the same throughout every hour of daylight. You follow the steps of Jesus to the point of his crucifixion through the streets of the old city. You can feel the climb. It becomes steeper and steeper and you can imagine the cross getting heavier for Jesus. It is a walk of faith, suffering, revelation and one which ultimately led to God's victory over sin.

No one can be certain exactly what route Jesus took but the established one trodden by pilgrims today is symbolic of that climb. The first station of the cross (Jesus is condemned to death) is opposite the Ecce Homo Church which is run by the sisters of Sion. This church has been built on the site that was once occupied by the Antonia Fortress. Slowly, you can follow the stations of the cross up the hill through streets where shops are selling everything imaginable. The noise of people, cars and animals and the smell of food cooking are all around you. The air is filled with the aromas of spices and herbs.

The climb eventually brings you to the Church of the Holy Sepulchre where the final stations of the cross are situated. The present church has its roots in the Crusader period. This is not my favourite place in the Holy Land: it gives the impression of Oxford Circus tube station at times. But there have been poignant moments over the years when the true meaning behind the symbolism of the place has been deeply moving.

The church which Constantine envisaged was much greater than today's version. There is little agreement between the Latin Catholics, Greek Orthodox, Armenians, Coptics, Syrians and Ethiopians about future development of the site. Inside the church you will find an anointing stone, a steep staircase up to the top of Mount Calvary and the final stations. There is an empty tomb, several caves and many altars.

I urge you not to be disturbed or confused by the mishmash of people and places inside the church. Try to remember that somewhere around this site Jesus' crucifixion took place. You will also probably feel very tired by now because you will have been walking for some time and the physical and spiritual demands can make you feel peculiarly exhausted.

Reading

They led him out to crucify him. They enlisted a passer-by, Simon of Cyrene, father of Alexander and Rufus, who was coming in from the country, to carry his cross. They brought Jesus to the place called Golgotha, which means the place of the skull. They offered him wine mixed with myrrh, but he refused it. Then they crucified him, and shared out his clothing, casting lots to decide what each should get. It was the third hour when they crucified him. The inscription giving the charge against him read, 'The King of the Jews'. And they crucified two bandits with him, one on his right and one on his left. (Mark 15:21–27)

Dame Thora reflects

"Now, I couldn't actually do this walk so I am relying on my daughter, Jan, to tell you a little bit about how it affected her. Certainly over dinner in the hotel that night there was plenty to talk about. Jan remembers her first Via Dolorosa like this:

AD 35 and the twentieth century really come together and hit you squarely on the jaw as you attempt to progress on the route of Our Lord on the Via Dolorosa. Every sense is stretched to its limit. Sights and sounds crowd into my mind where powerful emotions already occupy most of the space ... But I shouldn't start at the end of my experience, I should start at the beginning.

So let me go back to the evening before, in the Kings Hotel.

There was a definite air of excitement running through our little band of pilgrims. No one can truly prepare you for what must surely be an extremely personal experience for every individual, according to their own faith and how they journey towards God in their own religious belief. The Reverend Rob was on hand to share in the buzz of expectation that existed. There were practical things discussed too. To carry a small bottle of drinking water was one good idea that was to prove most welcome several times the next day, and to wear 'easy-to-remove' shoes or sandals (since Muslim places of worship demand the removal of footwear). And, on that same subject, socks are a good idea. They may not look terrific, but they do stop you getting blisters and enable one to walk on the rugs and carpets with a little protection against who knows what!

Several of the young female members of our group had already been embarrassed on the day we visited Capernaum. While we were walking around the grounds of St Peter's house they had been shouted and pointed at for not wearing long skirts. These sweet girls were only eleven or twelve years old and none of us had given a second thought to their tiny summer skirts and shorts – obviously a mistake. And even the next day in Jerusalem, although beautifully dressed in summer dresses they were, once again, to suffer being 'pointed out' because their skirts were above their knees. Fortunately, two long scarves were to appear from their mother's bag and were quickly wrapped around their slim young waists. I did feel for the girls. When you are in a group of grown-ups the last thing any young person wants is to stick out for any reason.

Another thing we discussed, very sensibly, on that evening was personal security. The lanes of the old city are so terribly narrow and crowded. One had to be prepared for a lot of pushing and shoving and therefore a serious danger of pick-pockets. 'Hold on to your wallets and purses as tightly as you do in the London Underground!' someone had remarked. And finally, there had been the shaming tales of some young Brits who had been claiming that their wallets had been stolen and who were asking pilgrims for taxi money to get to the British Embassy. Apparently they made a very good living from the unsuspecting tourists.

The day arrived. To no one's surprise it was a beautiful, hot, sunny morning. We drove to the Wailing Wall. I kissed my parents and waved 'Bye for now' as they took a taxi to return to the hotel, while the rest of us, slightly younger, slightly stronger folk began our walk through the Holy City.

The Golden Dome of the Rock came first, dominating any vista of the old city. Newly covered in gold leaf, it is a remarkable sight. It was paid for by King Hussein of Jordan, who, rumour has it, sold one of his homes in England to pay for it. It was well worth the removal of shoes to enter this most holy of Muslim places. We were asked to keep quiet as a mark of respect, a thing I was most happy to do in order to see the inside of this fascinating historical building. There are many Crusader features up near the roof which leads one to surmise that this was not always a mosque. While our guide was whispering these details to us I took the opportunity to lean against one of the series of giant marble pillars that run down each side of the centre aisle. I felt the cool of the marble through my blouse and was grateful for it. Our guide was telling us how King Hussein's father had

The Church of the Holy Sepulchre

visited Jerusalem on a peace-seeking mission and had been tragically assassinated. 'And, Jan, if you will kindly move, there is the bullet hole!' I jumped forward and, sure enough, exactly where I had been leaning, there was a bullet hole in the column. That chilled me very quickly, I can tell you!

We walked on to the Temple square which sits in a setting of great beauty. The amateur photographers among us loved this square. It is a wonderful setting. Inside the church I must admit to a strange feeling I get when I see religious commercialism on the huge scale of the things and places we are saving. And I recognise it is my own failing not to be able to identify completely with so many differing Christian attitudes and cultures. I suppose I had thought, prior to this pilgrimage, that I would feel 'at home' and immediately comfortable with any Christian culture, and of course this was not to be the case. In fact, as our pilgrimage progressed, I understood more and more what a very narrow Anglican view of my religion I had and that, in fact, what I should feel was that my Christian belief made me a part of what was, manifestly, the most intricate, colourful, multicultural faith in the world.

The Stations of the Cross

If I close my eyes at this moment I can relive our first station of the cross: our few brave voices singing over the noise of cheap radios, motor bikes, motor horns, people shouting; the feel of the uneven cobbles beneath our feet, and the constant pulling of our clothes by begging children demanding our attention all along the way; the fumes of diesel and petrol mixed with the smells of woodfires, cooking, donkeys and human waste. Large tears rolled down my face. 'He was here' kept going through my mind. 'He was here.' I pulled myself together. 'Come on, Jan,' I thought. 'This is just the beginning, you will never get through the day at this rate!'

I must admit to being in a rather unnerved state just before our first prayer. A few minutes earlier we had walked through a small courtyard-type square. An Arab, who appeared to be mentally handicapped, had shouted something to some young boys who had immediately picked up rocks and started to stone him. I realised we could do nothing in this situation and as local people started running towards the scene I quickly encouraged our group to keep walking. Since I was bringing up the rear only a few of my fellow travellers had seen what was happening, thank goodness, for I am sure it would have distressed them as much as it did me.

Yet, that very happening had emphasised to me more than ever how little had changed here since Our Lord's day. At the second station we visited the catacombs under the Convent of the Sisters of Sion. This was a relaxing break for my emotional tension. The small building was crowded with several hundred pilgrims, the majority of whom seemed to have wonderful, warm northern English voices! It turned out that at least one group was from Yorkshire and the sound of their northern accent was like a safe anchor in a storm for a few minutes before we returned to 'real life' through the narrow door and out into the hot sunlight and bustling streets once more.

At this point we were really lucky to have Reverend Rob with us. It was getting near lunchtime and he had promised us the city's best and cheapest pizzas. In a room no bigger than my kitchen at home, Rob was welcomed like family and fresh, delicious pizzas appeared as if by magic. Lunch was fast and soon we continued on our way. Station after station – up the winding street, climbing, stopping, praying, reading from the Bible and singing. Ever upwards, with ever growing thoughts and emotions, we worked our way through this amazing Holy City, my eyes taking in the myriad of colours in the street stalls and open-fronted shops. The massive amounts of souvenirs (each shop seems to sell the same things) were quite amazing! There was an infinite variety of monks and nuns from every country one can think of. Then came the strangely special visit to the tiny chapel of the Ethiopian monks on the rooftop with incense-laden air and monks in constant prayer, and finally our arrival at the Church of the Holy Sepulchre.

The Top of Calvary
My personal feeling upon reaching the top was intense. Curiously, I felt very withdrawn, with no desire to share the experience or speak of what was happening to me. There was no doubt that I was emotionally drained – yet, if you asked me, did I believe that the crucifixion of Our Lord happened on or near that spot, I can only say that, although everything around me seemed to be there for the sole purpose of making me sceptical, yet I believed. Our final hymn was sung in a small and dusty side chapel where we stood side by side in a circle on the dry dirt floor and sang 'Thine be the glory'. If there was one of us unmoved at that time, I don't remember: it seemed to me we were all sharing in a giant sense of love and faith. I was never so proud of our little band of pilgrims and felt a closeness that those early Christians must surely have felt for one another.

As a postscript to this extraordinary day, we stopped at a souvenir shop close to the walls of the old city before going back to the hotel. While we browsed, a young student-type girl came up to us. She was English. 'I have been robbed of everything, can you give me some money for the taxi fare to the British Embassy?' We pointed out to her that a couple of local policemen were walking up the street. 'They will surely help you,' we said. She was furious! As we walked towards our coach she yelled abuse after us, ending with 'you call yourselves Christians!' We looked at each other: 'Yes,' we said. **"**

Our Hymn

Dame Thora continues:

"Now I would have wanted to sing 'The Old Rugged Cross' but we didn't have the words with us in our hymn book so we sang this lovely Good Friday hymn instead. Isn't it great the way it sums up all that Jesus was prepared to do for us on that first Good Friday? On the top of Calvary he was nailed to the cross. What must Mary and his family have gone through? I think that you can only really understand the horror and sadness of it all when you have lived your own life. And Jesus endured that for me – and for you! **"**

> When I survey the wondrous cross
> On which the Prince of glory died,
> My richest gain I count but loss,
> And pour contempt on all my pride.
>
> Forbid it, Lord, that I should boast,
> Save in the death of Christ my God:
> All the vain things that charm me most,
> I sacrifice them to his blood.

See from his head, his hands, his feet,
Sorrow and love flow mingled down:
Did e'er such love and sorrow meet,
Or thorns compose so rich a crown?

Were the whole realm of nature mine,
That were an offering far too small;
Love so amazing, so divine,
Demands my soul, my life, my all.

(Isaac Watts, 1674–1748)

Prayer
Almighty Father,
look with mercy on this your family
for which our Lord Jesus Christ
was content to be betrayed
and given up into the hands of wicked men
and to suffer death upon the cross;
who is alive and glorified
with you and the Holy Spirit,
One God, now and for ever.
Amen.

(*Services and Prayers*, p. 199, *The Alternative Service Book 1980*)

12

Several Places and Little England

THE RESURRECTION

There are several places in the Holy Land where pilgrims can celebrate the resurrection of Jesus. The Garden Tomb is perhaps the most appealing, whilst the Church of the Holy Sepulchre is the most traditional. Another well-known site strongly connected with the resurrection is undoubtedly the road from Jerusalem to Emmaus. There are, however, at least three different locations for Emmaus which have, at times, been regarded as possibly authentic.

The most likely site of Emmaus, since the Byzantine

period, is at Latrun which is just past Abu Ghosh, about 12 kilometres away from Tel Aviv. The church, garden and small gift shop are run by French Benedictine monks who make you very welcome indeed. The acoustics in the lovely church are impressive and the gardens are exceptional.

As we were on the last day of our pilgrimage we left Abu Ghosh to return to Jerusalem for our celebration of the resurrection. The Garden Tomb is a popular site, away from the noise of the Holy Sepulchre Church, but we decided to go back to the Anglican Church for a final Holy Communion Service. We went to St George's Cathedral, which is on the east side of the city and which is run by the Anglican Bishop and Dean. The cathedral is well known for its pro-Palestinian stance. In the 1990s events have gradually demanded a more balanced approach to the political situation. The lack of consensus amongst the Jewish community is matched by that of the Palestinians.

St George's has a small guest house, a lovely garden, a bar and a dining room. In the church it was hard to believe that we were not in Surrey or Lancashire. It is so English!

Reading

Now that very same day, two of them were on their way to a village called Emmaus, seven miles from Jerusalem, and they were talking together about all that had happened. And it happened that as they were talking together and discussing it, Jesus himself came up and walked by their side; but their eyes were prevented from recognising him. He said to them, 'What are all these things that you are discussing as you walk along?' They stopped, their faces downcast.

Then one of them, called Cleopas, answered him, 'You must be the only person staying in Jerusalem who does not know the things that have been happening there these last few days.' He asked, 'What things?' They answered, 'All about Jesus of Nazareth who showed himself a prophet powerful in action and speech before God and the whole people and how our chief priests and our leaders handed him over to be sentenced to death, and had him crucified. ... Now while he was with them at table, he took the bread and said the blessing; then he broke it and handed it to them. And their eyes were opened and they recognised him; but he had vanished from their sight. Then they said to each other, 'Did not our hearts burn within us as he talked to us on the road and explained the scriptures to us?' (Luke 24:13–32)

Dame Thora reflects

❝We celebrated the end of our pilgrimage as Christian soldiers in St George's Cathedral, which is just on the east side of the old city. When we arrived we went to a lovely little courtyard where we enjoyed a drink and met up with the Dean. The Reverend Rob went off to put his robes on and to prepare for our final Holy Communion service.

St George's Cathedral is a bit like little England, in the sense that it is the 'Church of England' in Jerusalem. But you actually feel as if you are back in England – apart from the weather, of course. We left the courtyard and went into the cathedral where Jimmy, Jan and I were led to the front. Various people read lessons, including the story of the resurrection. There was no organ, so someone gave us the note and we sang some wonderful hymns unaccompanied. The prayers were a joy – we had a lovely time. We all shared in the service of Holy Communion.

It was in St George's that our hearts and minds focused on the resurrection of Jesus. The readings and prayers that we had heard on the Via Dolorosa really came back into sharp focus – the fact that he had defeated death and had risen again. When you read the story of the crucifixion or see a painting of it, the pain and sorrow of the whole event comes very much to the fore. You can see the pain and sorrow. But that was how far Jesus was prepared to go for us. 'Into thy hands I commend my spirit' is a wonderful statement of faith – and yet it is so sad that we allowed it to happen.

So can you imagine how Mary and the others must have felt? Jesus had not only died, he had been killed and had nails hammered through him. He had been crucified. He was placed in the tomb. They must have felt desperate, terrible, after what had happened. But that is why Easter is so special and so lovely, because all that sorrow and misery turns into joy and love again. A lot of people don't know that the rolling of Easter eggs reminds us of the rolling away of the stone from the tomb. We had seen the tomb of Jesus in the church and the Garden Tomb. It was empty: he is alive. New life was for everyone.

Knowing that 'Onward Christian Soldiers' is my favourite hymn, this was chosen as our last hymn together. I have known it all my life and, even though the words themselves are lovely, I think it is the tune which I love the most. We used to have it a lot on the 'Praise Be!' programme. We had all been Christian soldiers, following in the footsteps of Jesus. We had been pilgrim soldiers, working together to learn about how we can defend the gospel in our lives. The tune is quite theatrical – lovely, really. Marching onwards, together.

Looking back on the whole pilgrimage I do view life and faith in a different way. As I said before, I think every Christian ought to try and go on a pilgrimage. There's a saying that every actress ought to do a season in Blackpool because it teaches you a lot. Well, I think ever Christian should have at least a week in the Holy Land.

We do have good news to tell people and they do need to hear it when their lives become difficult. I receive hundreds of letters every month from people who just want to tell me how they are and what they are doing. People's lives can be very complicated indeed.

After a pilgrimage you see the Bible differently. The stories come to life. The distances between places become vivid and much smaller than you imagined. There is a wonderful atmosphere there and you bring this home with you. When I read my Bible or say my prayers my thoughts are often with me from the pilgrimage. Prayer is talking and listening to God. Often when I say my prayers I see pictures. And having seen the places and visited them, of course you have a better picture in your mind.

Whenever Jimmy and I talked about the pilgrimage when we returned we realised just how much it had affected us. It had impressed Jimmy very much – I know that. I thank God that he was able to visit the Holy Land before he died. **"**

Our Hymns
"We sang two hymns in the cathedral – without the organ, of course – which I still remember. My favourite – as I have already said – and then that wonderful Easter hymn of glory 'Thine be the glory'. You know that Christ is risen when you hear that hymn: you know that death is not the end – only the beginning. **"**

164

Thine be the glory, risen, conquering Son,
Endless is the victory thou o'er death hast won;
Angels in bright raiment rolled the stone away,
Kept the folded grave-clothes, where thy body lay.

Thine be the glory, risen, conquering Son.
Endless is the victory thou o'er death hast won.

Lo, Jesus meets us, risen from the tomb;
Lovingly he greets us, scatters fear and gloom;
Let the Church with gladness hymns of triumph sing,
For her Lord now liveth, death has lost its sting.

No more we doubt thee, glorious Prince of life;
Life is nought without thee; aid us in our strife;
Make us more than conquerors through thy deathless love;
Bring us safe through Jordan to thy home above.

(E. L. Budry, 1854–1932)

Onward, Christian soldiers!
Marching as to war,
With the cross of Jesus
Going on before.
Christ the royal master
Leads against the foe;
Forward into battle,
See, his banners go!
Onward, Christian soldiers!
Marching as to war,
With the cross of Jesus
Going on before.

At the sign of triumph
Satan's host doth flee;

On then, Christian soldiers,
On to victory!
Hell's foundations quiver
At the shout of praise;
Brothers, lift your voices,
Loud your anthems raise:

Like a mighty army
Moves the Church of God;
Brothers, we are treading
Where the saints have trod:
We are not divided,
All one body we,
One in hope and doctrine
One in charity.

Crowns and thrones may perish
Kingdoms rise and wane,
But the Church of Jesus
Constant will remain:
Gates of hell can never
'Gainst that Church prevail;
We have Christ's own promise,
And that cannot fail.

Onward, then, ye people,
Join our happy throng,
Blend with ours your voices
In the triumph song:
Glory, laud and honour
Unto Christ the King;
This through countless ages
Men and angels sing.

(S. Baring-Gould, 1834–1924)

Postscript

Some of the Wonders of the World

MASADA AND THE DEAD SEA

Dear Aunt Maud –
Had lunch in
Sodom and Gomorrah!
love T.
P.S. Bit salty.

POSTCARD

Aunti:
I Glebc..
Postletl..
DONCA.
U.K.

Any visit to Israel is incomplete without the day-long tour to the Dead Sea, Masada and Qumran. The Dead Sea lies 400 metres below sea level which makes it the lowest point on the earth's surface. It is called the Dead Sea because it only receives water – none flows out. It is full of concentrated minerals and salt (it has a salt content of about 25 per cent). In Madaba, across the border in Jordan, there is a fine mosaic of the Holy Land showing small fish swimming along the River Jordan very happily; when they see the Dead Sea ahead they gradually turn around and go back for fear of a salty death.

The sea is around 80 kilometres long and 18 kilometres across at its widest point. Its only source of water is the River Jordan and this is causing present-day Israel some concern because the level of the Dead Sea is falling dramatically, year by year. Even in the twelve or so years that I have been visiting the region the water level has dropped significantly as interest in the sea and its minerals has risen. The hot climate means that the water evaporates at a phenomenal rate. Israel trades heavily in potassium, calcium, magnesium and sodium, and Dead Sea beauty products are very popular indeed. Experts are currently looking at ways of bringing water from the Mediterranean.

In the Bible the region is most strongly associated with the stories surrounding Sodom and Gomorrah, towns which were destroyed because of the people's immorality. The story of Lot and the pillar of salt is a well-known one – and frequently referred to on pilgrim tours! (Genesis 19)

The Dead Sea road from Jericho brings you eventually to Masada. This massive outcrop of rock rises to more than 400 metres above the Dead Sea and is a natural fortress. But it was only used in this way for about a hundred years as a refuge for Herod the Great and then, most famously, as the place where the Jewish Zealots held out against the Romans in AD 73 for more than three years after the fall of Jerusalem. When Herod arrived there in 40 BC he embarked on a massive construction programme on the top of Masada. In the decade that followed Masada became a great fortress with walls, barracks, storehouses and cisterns. Here Herod was guarded by his loyal troops. The fortress could keep stores of food fresh for a long time.

A few decades after Herod's time, when the Roman Empire was spreading rapidly, a group of Zealots, led by Menachem ben Judah, came and settled in Masada. But during one of his visits to the Holy City Menachem was assassinated by a fellow Jew and his nephew, Eleazar ben Yair, assumed command of Masada. As the Romans closed in the Zealots made Masada as invincible as possible. In AD 72 the Romans surrounded Masada and, after a long siege, they decided to storm the fortress. But when they arrived they found no resistance: Eleazar had summoned his fellow Jews to die rather than submit to slavery and 960 bodies were found instead. According to Josephus, however, two Jewish women had crawled into a water pipe and lived to tell the story. The slogan associated with the site today is that 'Masada will not fall again'.

The visitor climbs to the top of the fortress either by cable car or on foot, depending on the time available, energy level and heat. It is usually very warm at Masada. It is on the way home, after the almost statutory float in the waters of the Dead Sea, that pilgrim coaches usually stop off at the Qumran caves where the Dead Sea Scrolls were found. The road was not built until the mid 1960s and the site has only recently become popular. The story of how a Bedouin boy found the manuscripts which had been hidden for almost two thousand years in a cave is well known, but the implications of his discovery both for our understanding of the period and for theology continue to be investigated.

Reading
Let our wives die without abuse, our children without knowledge of slavery; after that, let us do an ungrudging kindness to each other, by preserving our freedom as a glorious winding sheet. Come! While we have free hands and can actually hold a sword, let them do a noble service to us. Let us die without being slaves to our enemies so that we leave this world as free men in company with our wives and children. (From the funeral oration: Josephus)

Dame Thora reflects

"This was the most tiring day, but we didn't half cover some miles and we saw some of the wonders of the world – the fortress of Masada, the Dead Sea floating waters and the caves where they found the Dead Sea Scrolls. What a day!

Leon, our guide, suggested we left by 7.30 am so that we wouldn't have to queue for the cable car at Masada. I told the Reverend Rob that I wanted to go to the foot of the fortress and look from there, but Jan was determined to go to the top.

After about half an hour we caught our first glimpse of the waters of the Dead Sea. It was strange really, after Galilee, I mean you wonder what a Dead Sea will look like until you actually see it. And there was hardly any movement, just a heat haze and some white deposits near to the surface – obviously the salt and minerals which they use to make wonderful face cream, soap and cosmetics.

We travelled on, for mile after mile along the shores of the Dead Sea and quite a few members of the group had brought along their costumes so that they could have a float. Then, suddenly, there was Masada – not a site I was really acquainted with, but it is an amazing story and you can see why the Jews look to it as a sign that they will never again be anyone's slaves.

We arrived at the base of Masada and as soon as Spartacus opened the doors – my goodness, the change in temperature. We were at the lowest point, the very lowest point, of the earth's surface and it was so very, very warm. The group did a quick march from the coach to the queue for the cable car and they were all loaded in it within about fifteen minutes. Jan waved to me and Jimmy out of the cable car and shouted 'Rule Britannia' as it set off. They were up there for a couple of hours with Leon. We sat below with Rob, drinking orange juice and looking at the marvellous monument. After all our studies of the New Testament and thinking about our faith it was good to have a day to reflect like this.

We had lunch at the traditional site of Sodom and Gomorrah after the visit to Masada. Can you imagine sending Auntie Maud in Doncaster a postcard which says 'I had lunch in Sodom and Gomorrah'? But they have them! I had a lovely pizza and salad and they looked after us. The group then dived (well, not really, because you can't let the water touch your eyes) towards the water and they all had a jolly good float. It was very warm by now.

Then – and we were tired, I can tell you – at about 3 pm we were off towards Qumran where we visited the site where that young lad found the Dead Sea Scrolls. In his own way he had won the lottery, hadn't he? What a find! What a success. **"**

Prayer
Almighty God,
we thank you for the wonders of the world;
for the courage and faith of those who defended Masada;
for the discovery of the Dead Sea Scrolls;
and for this amazing mineral water.
Help us to accept your wonderful presence in the wonders
    of the world that you have created.
Through Jesus Christ our Lord,
Amen.

Useful Information

Further information about places referred to in this book can be obtained from the following addresses.

In the UK:
Israel Government Tourist Office, 18 Great Marlborough Street, London W1V 1AF (Telephone: 0171–434–3651; Fax: 0171–437–0527)

Tour organised by:
Fairlink Christian Travel, 12 Glendower Place, South Kensington, London SW7 3DP (Telephone: 0171–225–0555; Fax: 0171–589–6090)

El Al (Israel Airlines), 185 Regent Street, London W1R 8EU (Telephone: 0171–439–2564; Fax: 0171–439–2920)

Bethlehem
Bethlehem Tourist Office, Manger Square, Bethlehem (Telephone: 02–742591)

Cana

Regular services are held for the renewal of marriage vows. Local information is available from the Mayor's office. Telephone: 06–517741

Galilee

You can enjoy a spectacular presentation of the history of Galilee at: The Galilee Experience, PO Box 1693, Tiberias 14115 (Telephone: 06–723620; Fax: 06–723195)

There is also a small cafe and an excellent gift shop.

Jerusalem

Israel Government Tourist Office, 24 King George Street, Jerusalem (Telephone: 02–241281)

The Russian Orthodox Convent, with its famous onion domes, is well worth a visit on the way to the Garden of Gethsemane. Also on the Mount of Olives thousands of Jewish tombs can be seen.

We were unable to visit the site of the Garden Tomb which is an increasingly popular venue for many who wish to escape from the hustle and bustle of the traditional site of the resurrection. This was discovered by General Gordon in 1882.

At Bethesda you can visit the pools near St Stephen's Church and the marvellous Church of St Anne (John 5:2–17).

Nazareth
Tourist Information Office, Casanova Street, Nazareth
(Telephone: 065–70555)

National Parks
Israel National Parks Authority, 4, Maklef, Hakirya, Tel Aviv
61070 (Telephone: 03–6952281)

Sources

Thanks are due to the following for permission to reproduce copyright material: Petya Christie, for her work 'Was that my Gethsemane hour?' from *100 Contemporary Christian Poets*; The Central Board of Finance of the Church of England for four prayers taken from *The Alternative Service Book 1980*; Timothy Dudley-Smith for his work 'Tell out my soul, the greatness of the Lord'; Kingsway's Thankyou Music, PO Box 75, Eastbourne, East Sussex BN23 6NT, for 'Be still, for the presence of the Lord, the Holy One, is here' by David Evans, copyright © 1986; Lutterworth Press, Cambridge, for prayer from *Daily Prayer and Praise* by George Appleton; Maranatha! Music/Copy Care Ltd, PO Box 77, Hailsham, East Sussex BN27 3EF for 'Seek ye first the Kingdom of God' by Karen Lafferty, copyright © 1972; The Mothers' Union for prayer from the Mothers' Union Service Book.

Bible extracts are taken from the *New Jerusalem Bible*, published and copyright 1985 by Darton, Longman and Todd Ltd and Doubleday & Co Inc. and used by permission.

Photographs of the Holy Land courtesy of the Israel Government Tourist Office, 18 Great Marlborough Street, London W1V 1AF, and used by permission.

Sources

Photographs of the pilgrimage courtesy of Domenico di Barnardo.

The author and publishers have made every endeavour to trace the copyright owners of material appearing in this book. The publishers would be glad to hear from any copyright owners who have been inadvertently omitted and due acknowledgement will be made in all future editions of the book.